Some Well-Known People Who Endorse A Common Language . . .

"The gift of a common tongue is a priceless inheritance and it may well some day become the foundation of a common citizenship."—Winston Churchill

"The tie of language is perhaps the strongest and the most durable that can unite mankind."
—Alexis de Tocqueville

"Though representatives from many ethnic groups came together in the United States, English became their common language. Apparently, this was a natural choice. One can imagine what would have happened if members of each nation moving to the United States had spoken only their own tongues and refused to learn English."
—Mikhail Gorbachev

"English is 'the language of liberty' for nations emerging from years of cultural oppression."
—Vaclav Havel, President of Czechoslovakia

"A melting pot, yes. A tower of Babel, no."
—Saul Bellow, Nobel-prize-winning author

DEMOCRACY

OR

BABEL?

**The Case for
Official English
in the United States**

Foreword by Alistair Cooke
Introduction by S.I. Hayakawa

Sponsored by U.S.ENGLISH

Published by: U.S.ENGLISH
818 Connecticut Ave., NW
Suite 200
Washington, DC 20006

First edition, June 1991

Cover Art: FERST DESIGN

Materials in the chapter "American Success Stories", featuring Arnold Schwarzenegger were reprinted, with permission, from the following publications:
"I Wanted To Be A Champion", *Parade*, copyright © 1987.
"The Self-Made Man", *Premiere*, copyright © 1989.

Materials in the chapter, "Bilingual Education: Does It Work", were reprinted, with permission, from the following publication:
HUNGER OF MEMORY, by Richard Rodriguez, copyright © 1982.

ISBN 0-934833-05-2

ACKNOWLEDGEMENTS

In many ways, this book has been a collective effort. First and foremost, it could never have been written without the enthusiastic, generous participation of the many immigrants and educators who shared with us their inspiring stories and informed opinions about the process of learning English.

In addition, though, we must acknowledge an "invisible web" of friends and colleagues who painstakingly read through drafts, made suggestions, proposed clarifications —and, in general, made this book much more readable and internally consistent. These include Enrique Cubillos, Scipio Garling, Barbara Kaze, Katy Cusato, Angela McArdell and Debbie Mac Lean at U.S.ENGLISH, and Connie Wood at Clark Communications.

Needless to say, our wives and families were extremely helpful in this endeavor and gave much more than just moral support.

Last but not least, this book has seen its way into print through the kind generosity of more than 5,000 U.S.ENGLISH contributors to this project. Their names are listed at the end of the book.

To all a hearty thanks!

CONTENTS

FOREWORD

By Alistair Cooke

You may wonder why anybody, at this late date, is concerned about making English the official language of the United States. Until a decade or so ago, there never seemed to be a need to do so; we could take our common language for granted. Today, however, we see cities and communities filled with bewildered immigrant families. Some of their leaders say, "Wouldn't it be simpler to let people stay with their native tongue? Print everything in two languages. Let them, in time, also learn English."

This reverses an idea that is two centuries old, an idea expressed by the motto of our country: "E Pluribus Unum," or "Out of many, one." In other words, *one nation, indivisible.*

In 1937, the year I arrived in the U.S. on an immigrant visa, I visited a Bronx night school class where immigrant parents were learning English so that their children, first-generation Americans, would not be ashamed of them. It was a most moving experience, and it showed me how strongly these people wished to follow their children into a new life as citizens of the United States of America.

They recognized how essential it was to learn English *in order to become full citizens* of this country. They never thought of learning English as too difficult, or too high a price to pay, in order to enjoy the advantages this country had to offer them. They learned English gladly, and they went on to build better lives for themselves and a better country for all of us.

As you will see from the stories and anecdotes in this book, U.S.ENGLISH is not advocating that newcomers deny their roots or forget their native tongues. To celebrate the folkways, the festivals, the food of the "old country" not only enriches the variety of American life, but also adds a grace note to the solid tune of our Americanism.

But the day that the immigrant's native tongue becomes the first language of any community or—God forbid—a state, the American experiment will be in serious jeopardy of falling apart. We must not permit the divisiveness of Canada's language problems to become a part of our heritage. We must not reenact the nightmares I have witnessed in African, Asian, and Middle Eastern countries where a nation struggles to unite against the friction of competing languages and the violence spawned by ingrown hatreds.

As Nobel-prize-winning author Saul Bellow has forewarned, "A melting pot, yes. A tower of Babel, no."

Official language is not a new idea. More than 50% of the world's nations have designated a single language of government. Of course, this doesn't make all other languages illegal or keep people from speaking their mother tongue for private use. It simply means that for official business, *one* language alone may be used.

Please join me—and U.S.ENGLISH—in protecting and preserving our unity through one language. In the meantime, I hope you enjoy the stories of American citizens who came from distant lands. These people differ widely in almost every *way*, but they have one essential thing in common: they incorporated English into their daily lives with zest, joy, and gratitude!

INTRODUCTION

By S.I. Hayakawa

Our language has the power to divide or unite us. Words can drive us to war, or they can enable us to cooperate and to live in peace and harmony. From the perspective of my eighty-fifth year, I realize that much of my life has been dedicated to the assumption that cooperation is preferable to conflict. Throughout my efforts as teacher, writer, lecturer, college administrator, and elected official, I have had a continuing interest in the role that language plays in helping people turn potential conflicts into areas of cooperation. It is cooperation that makes possible all the achievements of our society, from the education of our children to the harvesting of food for our tables to the amazing achievements of science and technology.

In order for us to cooperate most fully with our families, friends, neighbors, co-workers, and fellow citizens, we must not only have language; we must have a common language. If we do not, our future holds a terrifying potential for conflict.

Let me explain, in an autobiographical way, how I came to this belief.

Early in this century, before I was born, my parents came from Japan to Canada, brought in part by my father's love of the English language and his dream of becoming a writer. Although he never realized that dream, his fluency in the language stood him in good stead throughout his life. At a time when many immigrant Japanese in Western Canada worked as field hands on farms, my father was able instead to organize crews of workers and negotiate their conditions of employment, because of his fluency in English. He also worked for many years as a traveling hardware salesman, work that would have been impossible without his command of English. Though he returned to Japan in the 1920s, to the last days of his long life he loved to read English-language magazines, newspapers, and books.

My own professional life has been full of surprises. After graduating from high school in Winnipeg, Manitoba, I attended the University of Manitoba and McGill University in Montreal. A faculty adviser once strenuously counseled me against pursuing an advanced degree in English, on the grounds that no school would ever employ a Japanese to teach English! (At the time, anti-Oriental sentiment in the United States was high, as epitomized by immigration laws excluding Chinese and Japanese—by race—from immigration quotas.)

Nevertheless, I persevered, earning a doctorate at the University of Wisconsin in 1937 and teaching there and at the Illinois Institute of Technology in Chicago. In 1952, the McCarran-Walter Immigration Act eliminated race as a barrier to immigration and naturalization. In a ceremony in Chicago in 1955, I finally became an American citizen.

About the same time, I was invited to teach a summer session at what was then San Francisco State College. The college offered me a permanent position in 1955. I must say I was surprised at such an invitation from a California institution, as I had known since my high school days that California has been, throughout its history, the principal source of anti-Chinese and anti-Japanese sentiment and agitation in the United States. After some hesitation, I accepted the job and moved my family. Happily, we have never had reason to regret the decision.

My teaching career centered on general semantics, the study of the relationships between our language patterns and our habits of thought—how the way we talk shapes the way we think, helping to make us crazy or keep us sane.

As president of San Francisco State during the tumultuous student strike of 1968-1969, I had a chance to see in vivid detail what happens to the process of education, and to the fabric of society itself, when cooperation fails and conflict ensues.

A few years later, the people of California elected me as their United States Senator. What had happened to the California I had read about in high school? This had been the place where aspiring politicians played on public fears of "the rising tide of color" and "the Yellow Peril" that would inundate the United States if the Asiatic hordes were not kept at bay. In the light of that history, it was astonishing that California was sending a Japanese-American to the United States Senate. No one was more surprised than I.

The roll of members of the Senate and the House of Representatives with whom I had the honor to serve reads like a miniature United Nations: Abourezk, Addabbo, Biaggi, Boschwitz, Fuqua, Gonzales, Hammerschmidt, Javits, Laxalt, Oberstar, Rostenkowski, Tsongas, Vander Jagt, Zorinski. Our governors have included names like Atiyeh of Oregon, Ariyoshi of Hawaii, Cuomo of New York, Dukakis of Massachusetts, and Sununu of New Hampshire—not to mention California's George Deukmejian, whose name is harder to spell than mine!

In short, America is an open society, more open than any other in the world. People of every race, of every color, of every culture are welcomed here to create a life for themselves and their families. This process has not ended; it continues as America embraces new immigrants and citizens from Vietnam, India, and Cambodia; from Ethiopia and El Salvador; from Paraguay and Pakistan.

We shall take them in, learn to live with them, and be proud of them, as we have done so many times before.

What will all these people have in common? What brings them into the American mainstream, despite their diverse origins and cultures? They will have learned English! Speaking English is the key to the possibilities and self-realization that American life has to offer.

In this book, Fernando de la Peña argues eloquently, from his own experience and in the words of many people newly arrived in this country, that new immigrants themselves realize as well as anyone the importance of mastering English. He explains, from his own observations and those of other teachers, the limitations of current methods of bilingual education so popular among those who advocate the establishment of a multi-language society.

Most important, Mr. de la Peña explains the ways in which language isolation can do economic, political, and even cultural damage to immigrant groups in this country. In his words, "Linguistic equality—the knowledge that you can speak with and understand others around you—contributes to political and racial equality as well."

President Theodore Roosevelt spoke to a problem that still threatens us today, as some people among us work to shift the focus of our society from the rights of individuals to the rights of groups: "The one absolutely certain way of bringing this nation to ruin, of preventing all possibility of its continuing to be a nation at all, would be to permit it to become a tangle of squabbling nationalities."

Today we see my native Canada riven by the dispute between speakers of French and English. India, Belgium, Sri Lanka, Yugoslavia, and the vast Soviet Union are all torn by factionalism, their many problems intensified because speakers of one language don't want to live or share citizenship with speakers of another language.

The miracle of the United States is that we have solved that problem. As the novelist and travel writer Paul Theroux has observed, while it is possible for an immigrant to become an American, no outsider can become, for example, an Englishman: "Foreigners are always aliens in England. No one becomes English. It's a very tribal society. . . . No one becomes Japanese. . . . No one becomes Nigerian. But Nigerians, Japanese, and English become Americans."

That we may speak to each other, understand each other, work together, and continue to build our nation; that we not be divided by barriers of language and culture into a separatist, sectarian society: these are the goals I had in mind ten years ago when I first proposed the English Language Amendment to the Constitution of the United States. These also are the reasons I helped to found U.S.ENGLISH, a national organization to espouse those goals.

The English Language Amendment says above all, "Let's see to it that our children, our young people, learn English. Let us not deny them the opportunity to participate fully in American life, so that they may go as far as their dreams and talents can take them."

Mill Valley, California, April 1991

I.

English Is My First Language Now!

Please allow me to introduce myself. I am Fernando de la Peña, and I am an American citizen. I love English because it has made a tremendous difference in my life and career. And I am so committed to its being taught well and thoroughly to those who want to learn it that I established an English-language school in Los Angeles, Cambria English Institute, in 1978.

I have written this book on behalf of U.S.ENGLISH, an organization whose goals I deeply share—and to which I am very grateful. U.S.ENGLISH helped infuse new life into the Cambria Institute because it is deeply committed to the aim of giving immigrants the best opportunities to learn English. I felt I could return the favor in part by offering the stories of immigrants (including myself) who have struggled with the English language—and come out winners! Perhaps more than any argument or polemic, these case histories are vivid proof of the strength of the human spirit in the face of daunting odds *and* of the importance of sharing a common language for the good of American society and for each of its citizens.

With your indulgence, allow me to proceed directly to the first story—my own!

My life has been in some ways typical of immigrants, in some ways not. Many of the details are different, but the broad outlines—the sacrifices, adjustments, and frustrations of making a new life and learning a new language—are virtually the same for all newcomers to America.

Perhaps the most important factor is the *age* at which you come to your new land. When you're younger, it may well be less difficult to make the changes, since there's not as much you must give up. I was lucky—I was only nine years old.

Although I was born in El Paso in 1936 and, thus, was American by birth, I spent my first eight years in Mexico. In fact, I thought that I was born in Mexico until my family came to the United States in 1944. My brother and I spoke no English when we arrived.

Two considerations made it seem advantageous for us to move to the United States. For one, there was a shortage of nurses in the U.S., and my mother, having received her professional training in El Paso (and being bilingual), could easily find a position. The second concern was our education. My parents decided our future would be brighter in the U.S., so we moved to Los Angeles.

Things weren't as rosy in the U.S. as I had imagined. We were a poor family living in East Los Angeles, with six to eight people staying in our matchbox house (an aunt and my grandmother lived with us as well). During the war, too, housing was a big problem, so my parents considered us lucky to have a house at all! My brother and I often slept on mats on the floor, but being an already tight-knit family, the close quarters only helped keep us together.

By December 1944, I knew I could speak English—not as well as others, or as well as I wanted to be able to speak— but I could make myself understood. (I've since found out that it takes young children about three or four months to gain this basic understanding.)

By the end of my first school year, I was among the top students. Of course, with my limited English, I had gone back two grades; I left my Mexican colony school in the fifth grade, but picked up in the third grade at Our Lady of Lourdes school in East Los Angeles.

From Our Lady of Lourdes, I went on to Cantwell High School, a private boys' school with 450 enrollment—mostly "Anglos". We were separated into different classes according to the results of an entrance examination. I noticed there were far more Hispanics in the slower tracks—but I quickly realized the separation was due not to discrimination, but simply to our lack of proficiency in English. The kids in the slowest room just didn't speak English as well.

In particular, there was a group of Hispanics from another grade school in a poor neighborhood in East Los Angeles who were the farthest behind. Some of these we called *pachucos*; they were Latino "zoot-suiters" with long hair, double-breasted suits, thick-soled shoes, and with very shiny appearances. They were from low-income families who spoke Spanish exclusively at home.

Linguistically, the *pachucos* were on the fence; they spoke *calo*, a mixture of Spanish, Portuguese, English, Italian, French, and a gypsy language. Even their own parents didn't understand the dialect they were creating!

There were different brands of *calo* spoken in different regions, so you'd have one type in East Los Angeles and another in San Pedro and a third in the San Fernando valley. The result was that many Hispanics became very provincial —we didn't have a common tongue to speak with or understand one another.

Many Hispanics like me had no problem learning English. We followed three simple rules: (1) Don't speak Spanish because the teacher doesn't understand it, and it would be impolite. (2) Don't speak Spanish because you're trying to learn English. (3) We are all trying to get along in this school, but if you speak Spanish, you are isolating other children who *don't* speak it.

We welcomed the opportunity to learn English. And we didn't feel we had to do it at the expense of our Spanish. I spoke Spanish the whole time I was growing up, and I never had to give up one iota of my Mexican culture.

I felt a lot of pride in my Hispanic brothers and in my Mexican-American community. As early as the seventh and eighth grades, I began attending meetings of the Belvedere Coordinating Council, made up of merchants and professionals seeking to improve the community. I asked a lot of questions and became very involved in the workings of this group.

On the other hand, this Hispanic pride had its limitations, especially when you took into account our limited English! Without a good command of English, many Hispanics wouldn't cross the Los Angeles River into the "other" Los Angeles. Many in our neighborhood could not make themselves understood with their *calo*. With only Spanish, many mothers couldn't shop over there, and "our" merchants couldn't do business with "Anglo" merchants.

So, even in my activism, I could see that English made a big difference. It was an essential skill in making your way outside your *colonia*, *vecindad*, or *barrio*—words expressing different notions of the idea of a neighborhood.

But *learning* English could be a difficult matter. My father, who wanted very much to speak English, had endless problems trying to find decent instruction. Because the teaching in the local nighttime classes was so poor, he ended up commuting three hours each day just to attend a daytime class in a high school across town! He learned a lot of English in this class—which was not a grammar or composition class, but one in *refrigeration*. (Since he already knew the subject, he could focus on the words—so it was an English course for *him*.)

My father's difficulties had spurred me to action. In addition, I began to visit a Mexican cultural activities center, called "La Casa del Mexicano", where I met one of my future mentors, Dionicio Morales. Morales was a social worker and activist who worked hard to get Mexicans to participate and be accepted by society at large. He trained recruits who would also become active in promoting the welfare of Mexicans. I was only twelve when Dionicio took me under his wing and began to influence my future course.

Dionicio spoke English extremely well. He had a tremendously effective oratorical style, through which he could make things happen. (He's still active today, serving as executive director of the Mexican-American Opportunity Foundation. In addition, one of the largest parks in East Los Angeles has been named after him—a rare honor for a living person!)

All of these influences, then—the Presentation Sisters of Our Lady of Lourdes, Cantwell High School, the Coordinating Council, Dionicio Morales, East Los Angeles, and the *pachucos*—opened up my vision. I began to see that English was a critical determinant in how my life would turn out.

At Cantwell, I got involved in the study and practice of oratory, or public speaking. Brother St. John, an Irish Christian Brother and another mentor of my early years, convinced me to pursue oratory; he devoted a lot of his time to coaching me, working with me on my English syntax, my writing, and my accent.

Brother St. John encouraged me to compete in oratorical contests. In my first contest, I gave a speech about the importance of the Virgin of Guadalupe in Mexico. It was very well received by everyone, and I began to realize I had some talent where speaking was concerned. So I entered more contests and began winning trophies. I even won a prestigious competition where the prizes were given out by Maureen O'Sullivan. It was like a dream come true, accepting a prize from one of the actresses I most admired! (You may recall her as "Jane" opposite Johnny Weissmuller's "Tarzan".)

My parents had taught me an important lesson: to expect that nothing would be given to us in this country. It was an important value to us, because the hand that gives is also the hand that can take away. Our family cherished our independence.

English made a difference in everything. I was asked to appear on live television and radio shows (including one with Steve Allen). Because I spoke English, and because I was willing to express myself, my participation was sought out. You couldn't participate if you didn't speak English!

When I went to college, I continued honing my skills in oratory. I had a speech coach at East L.A. College, Booth Woodruff, who inspired me to accomplish things beyond my expectations; and I began to realize that my oratory could be used to *inform* people of matters of great importance to their lives. I could also *influence opinion*.

I finished my college career with a major in Latin American affairs at Occidental College. Then I won a Fulbright scholarship to study political economy in Nicaragua. While there, I also taught English classes at the American Cultural Center in Managua. This was my first experience teaching English. I taught adults, who were good students, and the method I used, which stressed active communication, was particularly effective. I realized that teaching required a lot of preparation and sacrifice—and meant you had to be innovative, alert, sensitive to students' needs, and persuasive.

When I turned my focus to law, I was, frankly, a bit scared. In those days, we didn't have career days in school, and I felt at a disadvantage. I first attended Loyola School of Law, where there were only two other Hispanics in the entering class. All three of us were asked to leave by the end of the first year for academic reasons.

Many would be surprised that one of them is now a judge, while the other is a prominent attorney in Los Angeles. I say this only to point out that it wasn't that we weren't smart or capable. We just felt—and then acted—as though we weren't prepared.

In my case, when I got to my first exam at Loyola, where we were asked to write about a set of facts—what lawyers call "answering a question" or "writing an opinion"—I simply froze. I couldn't write a word on the exam book, not even my examination number, "96". My pencil just lay there and my mind was a blank. In June, I got my letter telling me not to register in the fall.

All three of us ended up at Southwestern University Law School. Southwestern at that time was a school for the working person, a one-building campus in the center of town, from which (I believe) every single mayor of Los Angeles and many local legislators have graduated.

When I took the Princeton law school entrance examination, I was surprised by how much emphasis the test placed on English. I kept wondering what English had to do with the study of law.

Law school turned out to be all about English! You fight with words, you try to convince people with words, you write words, you provide definitions of words. It's all words. Lawyers are scholars, orators, writers all wrapped up in one.

As I was finishing law school, the civil rights movement was in full swing. One effect of the movement was that many more Hispanics began to go to UCLA, Berkeley, and Stanford law schools.

An unfortunate side to this movement emerged—a trend that continues to this day. Some Hispanic attorneys began practicing in a fraudulent way at the expense of their own people. These lawyers had (and still have) an essentially *captive audience*: Hispanics who couldn't speak English and who relied completely on the services of these attorneys. In an effort to maximize their profits, these attorneys would then farm out the work to office personnel who may or may not have done the best job putting together a case for these poor immigrants. Again, I realized that the lack of English proficiency leaves you vulnerable.

When I finished law school, I got a job as a senior law clerk in the public defender's office. I fell in love with the job, because it meant I could directly help my fellow Hispanics. The office was headed by highly qualified criminal attorneys with a lot of commitment and ethical principles. My ability to speak Spanish meant that I could act as interpreter for the Hispanic community; my English meant I could communicate with the brass.

Of the 180 attorneys on staff, only five of us were Hispanic. On the other hand, a large percentage of the cases we got involved Hispanics who knew no English, and I was kept pretty busy!

One of the projects I worked on was a training program for kids in Los Angeles County. The public defender's office sent me to speak to these kids, particularly those with criminal records, and explain to them their rights and obligations.

My wife, Pat, whom I had just met at the time, accompanied me on several of these site visits and told me afterwards that I had made a great impact on these youngsters. "You should be a teacher, with the skillful way you have of explaining and persuading." Her words, spoken in 1970, were a turning point in my career.

In my own mind, I had always wanted to be a teacher, but I felt there were big roadblocks. Teaching was not a very exalted profession. Teachers didn't get paid well and were not considered to be professionals on a par with doctors and lawyers.

My parents discouraged my desire to teach. I sensed that my father would be particularly disappointed, which is why I went into law—not only to please my parents, but also because I felt it was the right thing to do at that time.

On the other hand, Pat had been a teacher for 10 years. She had a friend who taught an English-as-a-second-language class at night who was going away for an extended period of time. She asked Pat if she would take over the class. Pat declined, but suggested I do it.

I took it on. It proved to be a great challenge—but one I couldn't let go of. *In the very first minutes in that classroom*, I knew I was hooked on teaching and would never be able to return to my legal profession again. I would never become rich or famous, but I didn't care about those things—I was just having too much fun teaching to return to law.

It also seemed like the right thing to do. Law was important as a tool to help those in need in the community, but what people needed even more than that was English instruction. Through teaching English, I could have an impact *beforehand*—before their lives got desperate, their prospects crushed, and they turned to crime. I would make more of a difference to the community if I could *teach them English* than if I could get them out of jail.

The decision was hard, but it seemed inevitable. I was to follow my own path, clearly marked for me.

The first full-time position I landed was in a school where no one wanted to teach. It was called Central City Occupational Center Adult High School (now called the Abraham Friedman Occupational Center), and it was a "blackboard jungle" type of school—no windows anywhere in the 10-story building and students of the roughest character imaginable. My "kids" were all black and Hispanic, dropouts between the ages of 18 and 32. Most were around 18 years old, which, according to the L.A. Unified School District, made them adults.

I taught history and government—and a bit more, as you will see! While I was describing Columbus' discovery of America, I found out that many of the students didn't realize the world was round, so I had to embark on an explanation of earth science. These were not stupid kids by any means—there were some real diamonds in the rough among the motley crew of students I worked with. But I had to cover so much of the basic ground with them that I was teaching history only about half of the time!

The biggest deficiency that had to be made up at once was English, naturally. (The blacks, I discovered, spoke their own type of *calo*—so-called "black English".) Once I got many of these kids on my side, working with me and not disrupting the class, I drilled them in English grammar, syntax, and composition.

At the same time I was teaching daytime classes at Central, I had a night job teaching ESL (English as a Second Language) across town at a branch of Evans Community Adult School. Here, even though I was teaching only one subject, conditions were still horrible. Too many students were packed in a classroom. Often, I had over 110 students *attending* a class—not just registered! I never had fewer than 80 kids in my classroom. Only the L.A. Fire Department limited the number of people in each classroom.

In those days, schools had begun the practice of taking on too many students in an effort to increase their ADA ("average daily attendance") and get more government money for it. Even though I learned quickly how to turn this to the students' advantage, I was never happy with this bureaucratic way of computing a school's performance.

Here's one example of how *I* took advantage of ADA requirements: Because I wanted to see my Central City Adult students develop fully, I started a student government at my Friday class to give them practice in politics and oratory. Classes occurred on Friday morning, traditionally the day off for students and teachers at this school. My supervisors warned me I wouldn't be able to fill the class, but I managed just fine. I promised the students that, if they came to the morning class, we would pass the hat and, once class was over, we would reconvene at someone's house and have a party the rest of the afternoon. Attendance at the class was mandatory if the student wanted to go to the party.

Many of my students began finishing their high school work and receiving their diplomas within a year. The boys stopped getting into trouble; the girls weren't getting pregnant as often. I was named Teacher of the Year two years running.

I was very dedicated, very involved, very committed. After three years of this, though, I was also very tired.

I asked for and received a transfer for full-time employment at Evans Community Adult School in downtown Los Angeles, where I would be teaching ESL. The school accommodated 12,000 students in one small location. (Today, the school operates 24 hours a day, and over 90% of the students continue to be new immigrants studying English.)

The change was still welcome. I looked forward to the mix of students and the different challenges that teaching these students posed. I was, again, very successful with my students.

Things went along fine until 1978, when Proposition 13, the grass-roots movement to put a ceiling on property taxes, was put to the ballot in California. The school bureaucracy was so frightened at the prospect that they issued "pink slips" to all the teachers that spring.

Many of us were supporting families and couldn't tolerate this kind of uncertainty. A few days later, while stopped at a red light, I noticed an office building for lease. Suddenly, a "green light" went on in my head.

I went to look the place over and realized it had once been a school. There were still blackboards on the walls, and the rooms were the perfect size for small classes.

I talked to some business people, found an adviser and a partner, and on July 6, 1978, Cambria English Institute opened its doors for business. We were determined to make it work. If we failed, we had only ourselves to blame.

We started the business with $4,000. Half of that went to the rent, the other half to buy desks. We borrowed money for the paint and put the coats on ourselves. The school was opened with 18 teachers, two administrators, and two secretaries.

The first months were painful. By the end of July, we had only five students!

Our saving grace was that we learned fast from our mistakes, and we were able to quickly turn things around. For one, we had tried to make the curriculum extremely thorough: nine levels, with two months of study at each level. We soon found out that students wanted and needed preparation much faster than that, so we shaved the levels down to eight and the extent of each level to three and a half weeks. This way, students could complete the course in seven rather than eighteen months.

Since my partner and I had no money in reserve, we quite openly asked the staff to gamble with us. We knew this venture would pay off, and if they were willing to stay on, they would get paid in due time.

We didn't have to wait long. The following fall we had a streak of good luck. A Korean college directly across the street from us was having problems, and one day all the students and teachers just walked out—and walked right through our doors!

After that, every enrollment period we acquired 30 new students, mostly Arabs and Iranians, but some Hispanics as well. These were all visa students, meaning they were here specifically to learn English and would then return home to their country. Even though tuition was only $200, it was prohibitive to the new immigrant, so we did not have more than a handful of immigrant students here for years (basically, until the recent Amnesty Program).

We started night classes for the poorer immigrants in the area. I taught these classes myself. We charged as little as we could get away with, but it was still too much. There was such a tremendous need for these people to learn English, yet they couldn't afford it. But after trying a night program seven or eight different times, we saw that it would not really take off. We knew we would have to rely on the day program to keep the school afloat.

Business took a turn for the worse in the mid-1980s.

At Cambria, for the second time since we had opened our doors, we were looking bankruptcy right in the eye. I had to take out a mortgage on my house to pay the teachers' salaries and keep the school open.

We had always done a lot of marketing. For example, several of the Cambria teachers and I went to northern Mexico to give English classes and to appear on local television. We filmed several "live" spots for the news, which were broadcast on the only television station in the north. Many people saw us as we are in the classroom and heard our rousing speeches about learning English. These spots were very successful in bringing us more business.

But efforts like these still did not pull Cambria out of the fire. It took the help of a piece of legislation—and the kind generosity of a committed U.S.ENGLISH—to get us back on our feet.

Around 1986, because of declining enrollment, Cambria was in desperate straits. A few months after I took the first mortgage out on my house to pay my teachers' salaries and the overhead, the same crisis reared its ugly head. I again got a loan on the house, but this time many of my staff just couldn't handle the uncertainty, and many left.

I ended up with only three teachers who would stay. By this time, we were down to about 30 or 40 students (in our heyday we had had as many as 300).

A good friend of mine, Candido Palma, an alumnus of Cambria and a self-made man who had opened a burrito shop in Watts and was now a very successful restaurateur and landowner, gave me my first boost—without a hint of papers or contracts. He just handed me a large sum of money, with no strings attached.

The other substantial shot in the arm came from U.S. ENGLISH. The way U.S.ENGLISH came into our lives is truly miraculous to me.

When Cambria turned non-profit in 1987, we prepared and sent off between 120 and 150 grant proposals to various foundations, local and nationwide. *No one at that time even gave us the time of day*! My reading of this apathy was that English just wasn't a "sexy" issue like drugs, crime, the homeless, or unemployment. We had tried to argue that, if we could increase opportunities for everyone to learn to speak and understand English, we might make greater headway in coping with these "larger" problems. With the *basic* mode of communication in hand, we felt that social problems could be dealt with more effectively at the local level, without extra help. But our arguments fell on deaf ears. No one would fund us.

The miracle was that U.S.ENGLISH came to *us* unsolicited; we didn't go to it. It had learned of us through one of my former pupils, Mario Hernandez, who was gaining recognition for his offbeat, yet effective method of teaching English to Hispanics—over the radio! Mario had been my pupil in one of my beginning English classes and later in the "blackboard jungle" school, where he received his high-school diploma. After graduating from the University of Southern California, Mario opened his own English school and also began promoting English study in various new ways, such as this radio show. (Of course, many educators will instantly point out the limitations of such an approach to teaching language. Mario would not disagree with them, but the point was to stimulate increased interest in the community in language study, not to provide a substitute for intensive study.) When Mario was approached by U.S.ENGLISH, he told it to contact us as well.

Barbara Kaze, U.S.ENGLISH's West Coast director, told me that, if I could come up with an innovative program for teaching English such as Mario's, we could probably receive funding. We had been kicking around the idea of doing on-site training, so we put it in our proposal.

U.S.ENGLISH, backed by a generous grant from The Weingart Foundation, gave us a fresh start, from which we were able to make great progress. We not only got a one-time grant, but also a longer-term commitment to our English-teaching methods.

I will always be grateful to U.S.ENGLISH. I am particularly impressed by its members, many of whom I met at U.S.ENGLISH conferences held in Los Angeles in 1988 and in Washington, D.C., the following year.

As a guest speaker at the Washington conference, I got a chance to tell U.S.ENGLISH members that the immigrant was eager to assimilate and be part of American culture and mores. The members were very receptive to what I had to say. I could see that I had given them a ray of hope. Here again, I felt the value of English as communication—I was able to share many of my deeply held opinions with these educated, thinking people.

For example, I strongly believe in letting history speak for itself. The sagas of immigrants are a fitting tribute to the importance of learning English to thrive in and contribute to American society. Not only do the personal histories you will find in the rest of this book teach us that English is the cornerstone of participation, but the fact that these people are communicating their stories to us means that we share a common means of understanding.

It is my pleasure to share with you these inspiring stories of Americans who have made giant strides in their new country thanks to their commitment to learning English.

II.

Paper Tigers: Dispelling The Myths About Official English

First, let's take a closer look at some misconceptions about what might happen in this country if English were legally designated the official language. In any discussion of this kind, it is necessary to keep a down-to-earth and commonsense focus.

The issue before this great nation is simple: should the United States Congress designate English, officially, as the language of our government?

I should hope everyone would understand the wisdom of adopting English as the official language through a constitutional amendment. But, so far, opposition has been strong among certain political elements of the country and some ethnic leaders. Many trumped-up charges have been leveled at the "official English" movement. I want to dispel these one-by-one so you can see how false they really are—and how sensible and advantageous English as the official language of government is.

Here are a few of the charges:

MYTH #1: Today's immigrant doesn't want to learn English.

FACT: Not so! Immigrants understand that mastery of English is a necessary, basic ingredient of their adaptation to America. Asking one of these newcomers whether learning English is a burden or an imposition is a bit like asking them whether adjusting to new living conditions and new foods is unfair. Language shares with currency the feature of being common to all: it is a means by which people trade information or goods. People who don't have them are in big trouble. Most important, a knowledge of English is the number one key to economic well-being.

I've come to realize how wrong it is to think that all immigrants *want* to speak only their native language in the United States. In my experiences teaching in Los Angeles, I found that all my students wanted to learn English and participate in the affairs of this country. They want to be a part of society and understand what their opportunities are.

Asugman Atam, a dentist who immigrated with her husband from Turkey 14 years ago, feels very strongly about this: "I don't want to be different from others. Since I live in the United States, I want to be an American citizen and I want to speak English. At home, we still preserve our Turkish customs and heritage, but out in the world we try to blend as much as we can—and language is one of the most important ways we can blend."

MYTH #2: Language should not be made a political or legal issue.

FACT: How can it *not* be political? Those who do not have a voice cannot participate in the democratic process of this nation. If you don't understand English, you cannot comprehend what political candidates are saying and what their positions are vis-à-vis the issues of concern to you.

The President addresses the nation in English. Congress conducts all of its business in English. In order to have access to this information—and not merely rely on second-hand reports translated (and perhaps slanted) in another language —you must know English.

Indeed, full participation in the political life of the United States requires that everyone use common terms to describe the goals and ideals of American society. Even though it is possible nowadays to survive and operate in practically every large American city *without knowing English*, it is impossible to enter fully into the economic and political life outside your neighborhood if you don't have a good command of English.

Legal issues encompass all that we do in the public realm—all our dealings with others outside of our family and friends. In case you think it is a *luxury* to participate on this level, think about some of the compulsory "public" actions that require fluency in English.

For example, Dr. Atam, the dentist I quoted above, recently had to appear in small claims court. Although she speaks English quite well, she still felt her English was insufficient to present her case most forcefully.

"Because I was flustered and worried about my English, I realized only after the trial that I had answered some of the questions wrong, and others I didn't understand at all. I made mistakes that I regretted later—and basically lost the case because my English wasn't good enough!

"Even if I had had a Turkish translator in the courtroom, I don't think it would have made much difference. There's no substitute for being effective *yourself*—which means you want to be able to communicate directly with the judge."

MYTH #3: Official English discriminates against cultural or ethnic groups.

FACT: Not in the least! A recent Gallup survey discovered how immigrant families feel about making English the official language of government.

Almost three-quarters (74%) of families with a native language other than English were *in favor of* making English the official language. Even more of them (an overwhelming 88%) did *not* believe that making English the official language would unjustly discriminate against them.

A *San Francisco Chronicle* poll found that 90% of Filipinos, 78% of Chinese, and about 70% of Hispanics are in support of English as the official language.

The establishment of an official language will have nothing to do with whether other languages (and other cultures) flourish or die on American soil. These would coexist—as they traditionally have—alongside English in the private lives of its ethnic citizens. Whether the native languages would continue within an ethnic neighborhood or area is dependent on the vitality of the community and on the practicability or usefulness of these languages, not on a requirement that all of its inhabitants have a working knowledge of English in addition to their community tongue.

Also, the fact that a common language has been officially prescribed means that cultural traditions *can be* discussed and transmitted across ethnic and cultural barriers. Without a common language, separate cultures may be preserved only through segregation and cannot be understood by outsiders.

MYTH #4: An official language promotes cultural homogeneity and uniformity.

FACT: Doubtful—and without any historical precedent or proof. Official English will strengthen our common bond as American citizens, but it won't obliterate our individual identities.

The Gallup survey I mentioned above included the following question:

"Some people say that our public schools should be responsible for maintaining the languages and cultures that people bring with them to the United States. Others say that this is a private concern and not the responsibility of the public schools. Which comes closer to your view?"

Among families with a native language other than English, 64% felt it was a private concern—and not the responsibility of the public schools. It seems that most of these families see the preservation of their native languages and cultures as a duty to be carried out within the family, in much the same way that other "traditions" are passed from parents to children.

And precisely because an official language does not prohibit the use of other languages *in non-official discourse*, there should be little worry that it would affect cultural diversity. An ethnic neighborhood could continue to print its community newspaper in its own language, hold meetings in the shared mother tongue, maintain shops where signs and discussion are in the native language, and so on. No constitutional amendment could ever take that away, since it is a basic freedom of expression.

MYTH #5: Official English would cut emergency, health, and safety services in other languages.

FACT: Absolutely not.

In regions where significant numbers of people spoke a different language, emergency health and safety services would continue to operate in that language even with the adoption of an amendment proclaiming English the official language of the United States.

MYTH #6: Official English would require private business to operate only in English.

FACT: Official English does *not* require all business, publications, and television and radio stations to be exclusively in English. On the contrary, our Constitution guarantees freedom of expression—including the right to express yourself in any language you please. Even the passage of a constitutional amendment making English the official language of government would not alter this basic freedom.

But with every freedom come corresponding restrictions.

Certainly, store signs in Chinese will cater to the Chinese-reading populace—but how will these signs be interpreted by those who don't read Chinese? Is this sort of "market targeting" really beneficial to store owners, if many potential clients cannot tell what sort of store it is from the sign hanging outside the window?

While there is no *legal* impediment to putting out your shingle in any language you please, the act of doing so implies the people to whom you expect to cater. In other words, you are being selective about your clientele.

When many merchants and store owners opt to deal primarily in their native tongues in a given area, you have the phenomenon of "ghettoization", or a separation of the community from the outside.

MYTH #7: There isn't a current threat to English in the United States, so why do we even need an official language policy? Won't the numbers take care of themselves?

FACT: The problem *is* growing, from several standpoints.

The 1990 census figures have not yet been released *in toto*, but as of the 1980 census, there were 23,060,040 people in America who spoke a language other than English at home. (Of course, censuses often don't even reflect numbers of people who don't speak or understand English, so the actual number is most likely higher.) Many Americans speak primarily or exclusively a language other than English.

As our country's population becomes more diverse, there exists an increasing need for clear-headed leadership on the language issue. Without it, the problem will continue to be compounded as is the case with self-appointed ethnic leaders who use the "native language" issue as a significant bone of contention with the "powers that be". By treating language separatism as a top-priority issue, these leaders not only mislead their constituencies (who need opportunities far more desperately than their native languages), but they also misrepresent the intent and desires of ethnic minorities to the rest of the American populace.

Likewise, our federal government refuses to follow a clear-cut policy with regard to language use in the U.S., causing greater confusion. A Department of Education report on the 1984 National Association of Bilingual Educators Conference included the following assessment:

"With the exception of the Closing General Session, every General Session, Major Session, and Symposium advocated a greater role of the federal government in education, specifically bilingual education programs. Most speakers expounded at length on the need for, and the eventuality of, a multilingual, multicultural United States of America with a national language policy, citing English and Spanish as the two 'legal languages'."

More and more, we see our government accommodating newcomers to our shores in languages other than English, a procedure that is not only costly and cumbersome but is also divisive and lacking in vision. Shouldn't our government be promoting—and helping new immigrants to learn—English, so that they, too, might be able to participate equally and enjoy the many benefits our society has to offer?

This would appear to be a better solution, bringing all people together under the rubric of one language, rather than creating distinct islands or colonies of people who cannot understand one another without the aid of interpreters.

Many non-immigrants romanticize the lives of those who live in ethnic neighborhoods like Chinatowns, Greektowns, and so on. In reality, such strongholds of a culture can cause problems for their residents, if you look at the tough facts about ghettoization.

Of course, many immigrants like to preserve their traditions, customs, foods, and the like to give them a sense of the homeland they have left and to provide a feeling of community with other émigrés from the same land. This can be enriching to other Americans as well, who will visit these neighborhoods, patronize their restaurants, and buy goods in their shops.

But when these immigrants do not learn English and rely solely on what their small community can provide for them, it often results in the creation of a permanent economic and social underclass. These people will never gain many of the advantages available to them in the larger community— the United States as a whole. They are ripe for social unrest and become the easy prey of unscrupulous vultures from drug lords to religious leaders.

In my experience with the Mexican-American community in East Los Angeles, I have found some disturbing trends in the ways service professionals, political leaders, and religious authorities treat their own "people".

I told you earlier how the Hispanic attorneys often took their non-English-speaking clients for a ride. The problem has only gotten worse.

This phenomenon is by no means limited to Los Angeles. Recently in Washington, D.C., a large number of Salvadorans who had put their hard-earned savings in an investment company that catered to Spanish-speaking people each lost thousands of dollars when the illegal bank abruptly closed its doors. The company had advertised in the area's Hispanic newspaper (owned by the same man who ran the unchartered bank) but failed to mention that it was not federally insured. (Of course, many poor immigrant customers would not have known to ask about the availability of federal deposit insurance!) One advertisement had touted "favorable interest rates" for savings accounts—"favorable" turned out to be 3%!

Because these immigrants understood only limited amounts of English, they were a captive audience for ruthless schemes such as this one. In the process, many lost their life savings and possibly their hope of ever advancing in American society.

The medical profession has been another area of concern. In California, we have many immigrant doctors who will work for American physicians without having been certified to practice. Some get involved in dubious medical practices with their Hispanic patients with whom they speak in Spanish. Again, the lack of language is an impediment for which the immigrant suffers and may pay with his or her life.

Even religious leaders take advantage of newcomers to America. New fundamentalist sects are springing up that "speak to the herd"—and scour the pocketbooks of the faithful.

Last but not least, political leaders take advantage of ethnic communities where most people don't speak English. They purport to represent their interests, but who can really tell? Hispanics don't fully understand how the leaders are representing them to the American public, and English speakers don't know whether the Hispanics are feeling what the leaders *say* they feel. But Hispanics are like everyone else: we all have our separate opinions. If only we all spoke

English, we wouldn't need ethnic leaders to represent our views on our behalf!

A ghetto or *barrio* may look pretty and quaint from the outside. Indeed, life inside may not be so bad either. But without a knowledge of English, the inhabitants of these communities cannot reach for outside help; they cannot defend themselves against defrauding "compatriots"; and their prospects for the future will be limited by the boundaries of their ghetto.

A knowledge of English will enhance the mobility of the immigrant. It will drastically improve his chances to improve his lot: find a better job, shop for the best services, and know his legal rights and limitations.

But our government must take the lead, by declaring that all official business of government will be transacted in one language, our common language, English. This initiative will provide the impetus for the American people, "one out of many", to join together and move forward as a nation.

III.

American Success Stories: Profiles Of The Spirit

Most immigrants will tell you that learning English is one of the most challenging aspects of moving to the United States. So much depends on your being able to communicate needs and wants—and to make your voice heard on political and social issues of concern to all.

For the two men profiled in this chapter, there's an especially powerful twist to their language acquisition. Both use the English language extensively in their careers as actor and writer—so you could say language is fundamental to their survival!

No Grass Under His Feet!

How do you become an athletic legend, a multimillionaire businessman, *and* an internationally acclaimed movie star?

Well, you start by pumping iron and, then, learning English.

That's not as far-fetched as it may sound. English has

helped in the ascent of Arnold Schwarzenegger's rising star. And Schwarzenegger's story is an impressive one for an Austrian immigrant of modest background.

Certainly, making the transition from "farmboy" to champion bodybuilder to superstar actor requires extraordinary abilities. In Arnold's case, it meant, first, sculpting his body to truly Herculean proportions and, then, building his personality, his business acumen—and his language skills—to the point where they could translate to his ultimate goal: success in everything he undertakes.

He first became excited about coming to America while still in school. Film documentaries on New York, California, and Chicago "awakened something in my brain". He dreamed of something more than life in his small Austrian village, where everyone and everything were the same as they had been for hundreds of years. His family, while not poor, lived quite modestly. His father was a policeman who made enough to support the family of four, but there was little left over for luxuries.

Arnold's early years were difficult. He was used to getting up at 6:00 every morning, fetching the milk and doing chores until it was time for school, and coming home from school to do more chores and homework. Family life was traditional, regimented, and devoid of high aspirations or expectations. (It is reported that, when Arnold took up lifting weights when he was 15, in search of the perfect body, his parents considered briefly taking him to see a psychiatrist!)

But Arnold wasn't crazy—he just always dreamed larger dreams than his native village could accommodate. It was natural that he consider making the United States his home. America for Arnold was "bigger than life . . . I always wanted to come here".

At age 18, with a dozen European bodybuilding championships under his belt, he decided to emigrate to America.

After all, bodybuilding was essentially considered an American sport—the opportunities for training and competing were best in the U.S. But, in the larger sense, what attracted him most was "the freedom to choose". America meant you could do exactly what you wanted, as long as it didn't hurt anyone else. Arnold knew that, once he'd left home, he would return only as a visitor. On a trip home to see his mother in those early years, he cut his visit short; it had become painfully obvious to him that "I had much more the American spirit."

He arrived on American shores in 1968, with the contents of a duffel bag as his sole possessions. Almost immediately, he became "addicted" to America, as he tells the story himself. Opportunities in bodybuilding and associated businesses simply blossomed for him. While still in his twenties, he became a millionaire.

In those days, bodybuilding was not a particularly popular sport, even though it was practiced in the United States. It wasn't until the movie and book called *Pumping Iron* were released that bodybuilding began to assume greater respectability in America and throughout the world. This coincided precisely with the peak of Arnold's career as a bodybuilder.

After piling success upon success in the bodybuilding world, Arnold—to everyone's surprise—decided to pursue another path: becoming an actor. "I love being onstage, and I love performing. I was always ahead of the other bodybuilders because I was always more fun and entertaining onstage. I realized that I was really an entertainer, that I needed to develop another area where I could perform, and I made up my mind that it was acting."

As an actor, though, communication is perhaps the most basic component. You have to be able to communicate clearly, effectively, and convincingly to your audience.

No one wanted to believe Arnold could master these skills and grow to be much more than a muscle-bound Austrian farmboy. His first attempts to find an agent were pitiful. One agent told him to "stay with bodybuilding. You have an accent, a too-overdeveloped body for films, and a strange name that no one can pronounce." Another producer declared, "There is no possibility that this guy will ever make it in the movies."

It was the same kind of resistance he'd found when trying to make it in the bodybuilding world. But now, he knew that what people said to him didn't amount to a hill of beans. If he set about it in the right way and devoted his boundless enthusiasm to learn and improve whatever he undertook, he would surely succeed.

"I just went after it—acting. I knew it could happen if I worked on my talent and my accent, to make it understandable, and I thought eventually some people would learn to spell my name and even pronounce it. . . . Do you forget Gina Lollobrigida?"

He set about polishing his image and acquiring the sophistication that had not been a part of his upbringing. A close friend said that, in the early days, "he didn't know how to dress or order from a menu—things like that." But he asked people what and where to eat, what books to read, what hotels to stay in, where he could find a good tailor. It wasn't long before he had developed a spit-and-polish, supremely sophisticated look.

More than anything else, Arnold's cleverness and risk-taking seem to have been the factors that made his dreams come true. In the mid-1970s, Lucille Ball spotted him on the *Merv Griffin Show* and asked him to be a guest in a special she was producing.

Perseverance, the desire to tap every ounce of talent he had, and hard work paid off, perhaps not immediately but eventually. In his first movies, his roles were restricted, the dialogue severely limited because of his English, his "acting" involving more muscle-flexing than character development. In one film, his voice had to be dubbed over.

Just as his muscles had given him an entree into the movies, so they were also a drawback to his being given serious roles. It was clear that, without a thorough command of the language, Arnold would make money and movies only if he took off his shirt.

Gradually, his English improved and his acting skills developed—all with the help of numerous teachers and coaches. Arnold was now able to appear in a wide variety of roles in movies such as *The Terminator, Twins, Total Recall,* and now *Kindergarten Cop.* From a muscleman to a dramatic and comic actor, Arnold has accomplished in the acting arena what many aspirants have only dreamed of. His financial success is overwhelming: he now commands fees of about $10 million per picture!

Arnold is deeply grateful to America, its people, and its way of life. He has an enormous silk stars and stripes hanging across one wall of his office—that's how passionate he is about America.

As a businessman and investor, Arnold has also been immensely successful. He reportedly earned $43 million from his ventures in 1988 and 1989 alone. *Forbes* magazine lists him as one of the ten wealthiest entertainers in America.

But without a solid command of English and a strong drive to be accepted as an American, Arnold could never have reached this pinnacle of success. He became a citizen in 1983 and has been very active in national politics, most recently in George Bush's presidential campaign. He is currently serving on the President's Council on Physical Fitness and is involved in a number of political and charitable causes.

Arnold is also a distinguished member of U.S.ENGLISH's

Advisory Board. "I feel, and have always felt, that English should be the official language of the United States and that individuals who do not speak the language should be given all the assistance they need in learning it."

That, in a nutshell, is one of the "secret ingredients" in the success of Arnold Schwarzenegger, a truly American phenomenon.

Let His Fingers Do The Writing!

Did you know that the slogan, "Let your fingers do the walking", used for decades to promote the telephone yellow pages, was created by a man who knew virtually no English when he arrived in New York City in the mid-1940s?

This same man went on to publish 21 books and more than 200 articles, and to create breakthrough print and television advertising campaigns for major businesses. His name is Stephen Baker, and he's a man who learned early (and well) how to survive by his wits.

"America is my big classroom. I've been studying the language and the culture of Americans for decades—it's fascinating and completely absorbing to me." Stephen's love of all things American has been a long, inexhaustible affair. He has contributed a great deal to American culture—and has been richly rewarded for his efforts.

Stephen Baker has always possessed determination, strength of character, and ingrained survival instincts. Still, you would hardly have guessed that this Hungarian immigrant who stepped off the boat from Europe with $7 in his pocket and a carry-on suitcase filled with clothes—the sum total of his worldly possessions—would, with a little time, become a prosperous American celebrity.

He was in his mid-20s when he arrived. He already knew two languages—German from his earliest years in

Vienna, then Hungarian, learned after his family moved to Budapest when he was five. "Learning a new language when you're an adult is quite different—and quite a bit harder—than when you're a child. Whereas it only took me a year or two to get comfortable with Hungarian as a child—to 'blend into the scenery,' so to speak—it wasn't nearly as easy, at 20, to try to learn English."

Certainly Stephen's survival instinct had a lot to do with his rapid assimilation. "From day one in New York, I never thought of myself as a Hungarian. I was a man without a country, trying to make out. My entire ambition, my dream was to become completely Americanized."

To begin with, though, Stephen knew *not one word* of English. Once, when his shoes were falling apart, he took them to what looked like a cobbler's shop: "I held up my feet and I pointed at the hole in my sole. I gave him my shoes and then, of course, I thought, 'My God, this will cost me!'—some enormous sum of money. We didn't talk money. He just took the shoe. But when I reached in my pocket, he wouldn't accept anything!"

He encountered the same kind of generosity with a dentist. Stephen's tooth gave him more than one sleepless night. He finally decided to seek help. Sitting in the dentist's chair, he pointed at the culprit tooth; the dentist filled it for free. It was through these early experiences that Stephen came to recognize the natural warmth and kindness of Americans toward newcomers to the country.

Stephen attributes his picking up the language fairly rapidly to his dogged resolution to learn. "I wasn't particularly adept at languages. Believe me, I'm no intellectual. But I have always been result-oriented, I guess. Success was important in my family. My father would not ask, 'What did you do?' He wanted to know, 'What did you *accomplish*?' "

In his first year, he acquired between 500 and 1,000

English words—enough, he says, to conduct a "reasonably intelligent conversation." He learned by listening to people and, in particular, by going to movies. He would sit before the screen, often with his eyes closed to concentrate on the sound. Gary Cooper was his favorite actor, his drawl a focus of attention. John Wayne came in a close second. He tried imitating their speech but, by his own admission, with mixed success. "Midwestern twang and Hungarian just don't blend naturally," he says.

Although he arrived with his family (two brothers, his mother, and stepfather), it was only a matter of weeks before Stephen struck out on his own (as did his brothers, all of whom are also prospering today). Stephen doesn't recommend making your way alone like he did, without family or other resources to get you through the rough spots. Yet, he acknowledges that his solitary journey might have contributed to his getting used to the ways of America. "You're forced to strive for language skills even more when you're on your own. I had nobody—which was good and bad. It's bad because it's a hell of a lot of work. It's good because your options are limited. There's no shoulder to lean on. Not only do you live and learn—you learn and live!"

Stephen lodged in a YMCA-type dormitory, looking for work but finding limited success for his lack of English, when someone told him about the Hungarian Pavilion at the World's Fair then being held in New York. He thought he might get a job in the restaurant in the Pavilion, so he headed in that general direction, suitcase in hand.

He remembered that in Budapest he had always walked from one place to another. Distances were usually not great; they could be covered on foot. He assumed the same held true in New York. He soon found out differently. The Fair was in Queens—and it took him more than a day to walk there! He arrived late at night, when the Fair gates had already been locked, so he waited until the next morning. He got a job washing dishes in the restaurant and found a place to stay with a Hungarian family.

Stephen didn't get much practice speaking English, as the cook and his staff carried on spirited conversations across the kitchen in—alas—Hungarian. However, the World's Fair grounds gave Stephen a window of opportunity to learn about the culture of his newly adopted country. Seven days a week, in his free afternoons, he would canvass various exhibits, watching their audio-video presentations over and over again. He was particularly fascinated by a movie about the settlement of the American West, which he claims to have watched more than a dozen times. He had seen cowboys before, but they spoke dubbed-in Hungarian; this was the first time he heard them speak in their native tongue!

After a time, Stephen felt he could better himself—and his chances of learning English—if he were away from his Hungarian compatriots. He realized that the best way to learn the language and become assimilated to the American way of life was to surround himself with Americans in an English-speaking environment. After about a year in New York City, where the temptation to socialize with only Hungarians became too great, he struck out westward, where he figured he would have no choice but to speak English.

He went to work in the oil fields of Oklahoma by day, and by night he tried to finish high school, a process that was interrupted when the family came from Hungary. In one of his classes, he met one of the most important people in his life: his English teacher.

"She was a very good-looking young lady, which helped get my attention at the time. I was speaking reasonable English but certainly not fluent, and she would take out two hours every day for months to give me private English lessons—for free. She gave me a lot of confidence."

Stephen had struck out for the heartland of America partly to get to know more about what there was outside New York City, and partly because he was determined to get a college degree. There were no scholarships and grants at the time that Stephen could take advantage of. He found a small college near Liberty, Missouri, that would accept him, give him free room and board and an opportunity to work his way through school—setting type in a printing shop and helping in the kitchen of his fraternity house.

Stephen recalls the curiosity of college friends over his "cosmopolitan background". He surmises: "I must have seemed like a visiting alien to my new friends." The powers-that-be of the school put Baker on the football team for purposes of publicity: "Hungarian plays football." The media took to the idea—even if his coach didn't! It took this newest member of the team quite a while to decipher the complex rules of the game and to impress on his mind that American football had little to do with its European namesake. "There were many occasions when I would use my feet instead of my hands."

His new Midwest surroundings gave him a thorough taste of Yankeedom. "There was hardly a foreigner among the 2,000 or so people I met—a fortuitous circumstance for any immigrant determined to learn about his new country."

There was still "baggage" that he had brought from his Hungarian past, which took several years to shake off. For a long time, Stephen carried with him a fear of authority. "Just about anybody wearing a uniform would fill me with trepidation—including doormen and postmen!"

At what point did he begin to feel comfortable with his English? It wasn't until his third year in the United States: "I remember one morning when I woke up thinking about last night's dream. In this dream—surprise, surprise!—I was speaking to members of my family in *English*! This was a very happy moment for me. For the first time I discovered that I was actually *thinking* in English. I had champagne for breakfast that day."

Ever curious, Stephen traveled all over his new land during his summer vacations—without a car. He covered more than 40 states either by hitchhiking or by riding the rails. And, even though he did this purely for his own personal fulfillment, his observations and photographs soon found their way into print. "How To Ride The Rails" was his tongue-in-cheek "how-to" traveling guide to jumping freight cars, with elaborate notes on freight train schedules, meal planning, types of boxcars, and getting off trains unceremoniously.

Stephen's first published piece, though, was entitled "What's Wrong With American Women." It consisted of his own perceptions of American women, written in unidiomatic, ungrammatical English. Stephen figured if the article were accepted, they could clean up the grammar. Lo and behold, the four-page article was printed word-for-word in a local newspaper. "My first article had an accent! I sounded just like me." Later, the same article appeared in *Charm* magazine, this time in a more polished form.

Up to this point, Stephen had rarely entertained the notion of writing professionally. That was too much to hope for. He enjoyed traveling, writing down his thoughts and observations to share them with anyone interested. He became a regular writer/illustrator of *Ford Times*, a travel magazine aimed at the automobile crowd. Pieces for *Parade* and *Holiday* followed. "It didn't take me long to figure out that writing was a quicker way to fortune than washing dishes."

While it is true that he took to writing like a duck to water, Stephen is the first to admit that his life as an author was anything but easy. "Writing in English comes even harder for a non-native. Finding just the right expression, the one-and-only word is a real effort for me—still. You could say all my books are copies of various dictionaries on my desk. All I do is rearrange the entries."

His travels finally brought him back in New York City, his original launching pad. He tried to find a job in advertising. His positioning himself as a "promising copywriter" was greeted with notable lack of enthusiasm, however. ("Whoever heard of a copywriter who spoke halting English?") But the sketches in his travel scrapbook and published pieces were impressive enough to land him an assistant art director position in a few days.

Less than five years later, he was an art director with a unique ability (for art directors of that era) to verbalize his thoughts. Twice he was nominated as Art Director of the Year. He published several books on advertising art and design; his *Visual Persuasion: Effect of Pictures on the Subconscious* and *Systematic Approach to Advertising Creativity* are considered definitive texts and used worldwide. His books helped launch Stephen on a highly successful and visible career in advertising that took him to some of the largest agencies and "blue-chippest" accounts in the country. He was a columnist at *Advertising Age* for over a decade and collected more than 60 major awards for creative excellence.

"Being an immigrant actually helped me in advertising. When you step into a new culture, you pick up a lot of information that you may ignore otherwise. I am totally intrigued by American culture and the fact that the country has become the Pied Piper of the world today. I read the *New York Times* for breakfast every day and have never missed an issue for the past 25 years. I lecture on changing trends in America, shifts in taste and lifestyles. To tell you the truth, I guess I'm still that proverbial kid in a toy shop!"

Although Stephen has published 21 books — in six-figure print runs most authors and their publishers only fantasize about — he doesn't consider himself an "accomplished" writer. "My education isn't that good. I'm not a terribly good writer. But I've done it long enough to have picked up a thing or two. As an advertising practitioner, I pay close attention to the needs of the marketplace—and that is certainly a step in the right direction. Besides, the best way to learn about a subject is to write a book about it!"

Stephen never had fame and glory in mind when he wrote his books. The idea for his first, *How To Live With A Neurotic Dog*, grew out of his advertising experience. "I wanted to do a book that could prove to be *commercially* viable. It's not easy to write books after a full day in the office; I had no intention of indulging myself. My advertising expertise and marketing background told me that a title combining the magic words 'how to', 'dog', and 'neurotic'— words that touch a nerve—would find an audience. The concept worked. Everything else fell into place, including one other book on dogs, four on cats—two that became best sellers. You could say that my beloved pooch launched my book writing career."

Did he ever own a cat? "No, I never did. But I did borrow one for four weeks. Research, you know." A number of his books have made the permanent "backlist", the ultimate goal in publishing. His *How to Play Golf in the Low 120's* is one, celebrating its 29th Anniversary Issue. It is among the top ten best-selling books on golf and "it doesn't teach you a thing!"

Stephen has also become a consummate promoter of his own work, a rarity among writers given to introspection. "It's very difficult for a creative person to go out and meet the world halfway. It requires a different temperament. But I figure if the project has merit, I should be able to sell it. I'm the best person to answer publishers' questions—because if I don't know my own book, who does?" Stephen has yet to work with an agent to represent him.

In the past 20 years, Stephen has picked up a habit that has allowed him to improve his vocabulary dramatically: he reads dictionaries cover-to-cover for fun. "I've read five dictionaries so far, anything from Oxford to Contemporary American Slang. I spend 10 minutes each morning, reading a page or so while I sit and shave. It gives me a good reason to jump out of bed!"

But he's still modest about his accomplishment and feels it's unnecessary to use big words or archaic expressions when there's a perfectly good, simple word in common usage that will do the job. He sees this as a key to salable writing—convoluted multiloquence may prove to be an interesting experiment, but it is ultimately self-defeating.

For example, his *How To Live With A Neurotic Dog* contains only 626 different words. Asked on a radio interview about his penchant to economize on words, Stephen jokingly told the interviewer that he had no choice in the matter—the words represented the extent of his vocabulary.

That vocabulary has brought this talented man full circle since his arrival in the United States. Stephen recalls working on an account for an Italian ocean liner—the very same ship he took to America ten years earlier. At the request of the client, he and his advertising team took a short cruise around New York harbor to better understand a passenger's point of view and to be inspired to come up with creative ideas to advertise the cruise ships.

When the ship was returning to harbor, Stephen quietly broke away from his companions to go to the upper deck and stand precisely at the same spot he stood catching his first glimpse of New York City on his arrival from Hungary. The experience proved to be an eloquent reminder of his not-so-distant past. "I was very moved. America is indeed the land of opportunity. Now I was traveling first class—as opposed to the first time I saw New York, when I was but one of the hundreds of refugees coming out in the open from steerage. Then, I had only a few dollars in my pocket; today, I was an advertising executive enjoying the perks of my profession with plenty of money to spare. So there's always hope!"

Does Stephen miss his native Hungary? "Not really, because I've never been one to keep looking back. Coming to America was a new life for me, and a very fulfilling one at that. I was starting all over, fresh, and I'm doing fine, thank you. Forget the *qulyas*, give me a hamburger!"

IV.

Towers Of Babel

Can you imagine living in a nation where you cannot speak to your neighbors?

How important can your voice be if political affairs are conducted in a language you don't understand?

We know that, over the years and centuries, linguistic and national borders have not neatly coincided, giving rise to a number of "unnatural" or difficult compromises. Let's take a look at the experiences of other nations that have a multitude of language groups.

In India, for example, politics and business are transacted in more than a dozen languages, depending upon the region of the country and the prevailing language or languages spoken in each. Dinesh Desai, now an American citizen living near San Francisco, has had a lot of personal experience with language problems in India. Born there in 1939, Dinesh grew up in the cosmopolitan city of Bombay, where many different groups of Indians, each with their own language or dialect, live side by side *but have relatively little contact with one another!*

"My native tongue was Gujarati. At school, all my friends spoke Gujarati. We just didn't make friends with others—those who spoke Marathi, Hindi, or any of the other languages spoken right around us. You were limited to those who shared your language."

By the time Dinesh got to college, most of the instruction was in English. However, because lectures were the norm and class participation was minimal, Dinesh and his fellow classmates got little practice in speaking English. Outside the classroom, the groups of students who spoke the same mother tongue tended to stay separate and speak in their native language.

"India is really not a single country, but a 'subcontinent' unto itself—a conglomeration of different states, each with its own distinct language or languages," says Dinesh. "Some of the languages are related, so you can often understand others speaking to you, but you can't read or write in their language.

"India reminds me of Europe in one crucial sense: most Europeans share a common culture and a similar heritage, but each country has a different language. Of course, in Europe, each state has its own set of laws and its own government. Romania can act on its own, independently of what happens in England or Germany.

"In India, however, the states are not independent of one another, so the fact that a different language is spoken in each creates an extremely frustrating situation. It's hard to work together when you don't understand one another!"

As a result of the language differences, the democratic process in India can often be an utter mess. Particularly in cosmopolitan cities like Bombay where inhabitants speak any number of different languages, political candidates have to jump through linguistic hoops to reach a wide audience. They might speak their native language to their own people, English to another group, Hindi to a third, and so on. This is, at the very least, an inefficient way to conduct a political campaign. At worst, it's bound to cause confusion and misunderstanding.

Dinesh tells an interesting story of a "misfired" communication between regional governments in the south and north of India. "Between northern and southern states, language variations can be radical and unrecognizable. Recently, the Chief Minister of Uttar Pradesh (a northern state) wrote on official business to the Chief Minister of one of the southern states. He wrote the letter in Hindi, which is the language in widest circulation in Northern India.

"The southern Chief Minister couldn't make heads or tails of the letter. He didn't understand Hindi at all, so he had someone write a response in *his* native language, which is Malayalam, as well as a bit of English thrown in for good measure.

"Needless to say, the business took quite a while to sort itself out and get taken care of. They wrote back and forth numerous times before they could agree on the *terms* of what they were talking about!

"But this is no laughing matter, really. This is an extremely important factor contributing to inefficiencies in government in India."

In many ways, India is in a no-win situation. Currently, Hindi is considered the national language for all of India, and yet, in the southern states, Hindi is neither accepted nor spoken by most people. Languages in the south of India (Dravidian) bear little resemblance to Hindi, so there is little incentive to learn Hindi, particularly if you plan on staying in your own state among your own people.

Dinesh Desai feels that the only reason this patchwork linguistic situation works as well as it does—and doesn't cause the political and economic systems to collapse totally —is that India is at such a low level of industrialization. As long as most people are glued to their plots of land or living as peasants and piece workers, there may be no real need for India to adopt a common language for its 800 million inhabitants.

Yet this same fragmentation is preventing the people of India from rising above the most basic agricultural level, economically and socially. If they hope to achieve a higher standard of living for its people and create more opportunities for industrialization, India must adopt a common form of communication, so the resources and people needed for progress can be marshaled and harnessed to the same task! A common language would undoubtedly provide the first step toward this unification.

As Dinesh says, "Communication is the *basis* of any society. If you don't have communication in common, you can never have more than superficial dialogue. That isn't the basis of anything!"

Canadians, too, are at an undesirable crossroads: Quebec, because it wishes to preserve a monolingual (French) society and culture, is prepared to secede from the other nine English-speaking provinces. The country officially adopted a bilingual political system in 1969, giving French and English equal status.

The public expense of maintaining government services in two languages has proven staggering. In Canada at the federal level, it is estimated that it takes $1.3 million *every day* to duplicate services, forms, and other communications in a second language.

(To understand what this might mean for the U.S., first adjust this figure for the significantly larger population of the United States and its federal government, then consider that 148 of the world's 208 languages are spoken within our borders. Wouldn't we have to provide these costly services for all language minorities, if we provided them for even one additional language?)

A mere five years after Canada's bilingual status was established, the province of Quebec adopted French *only* as its official tongue. This has caused deep division and resentment from Quebec's English counterparts, who continue to comply with the bilingual statute. This divisiveness now threatens national unity.

Fans at Toronto baseball games jeer when the French portion of the Canadian national anthem is broadcast. Quebec officials have made it illegal for stores to post signs in English. English-speaking Canadians have defiled the Quebec flag—and vice versa.

Canada's bitter crisis of government focuses on the linguistic separation of French- and English-speaking citizens. Unfortunately, Canada is not an isolated case. The Flemish-speaking population of Belgium, while it has increased in economic strength in relation to the nation's French-speaking population, has lagged behind it in social and political rights. Friction and unrest have become the norm.

In countries such as Switzerland and Yugoslavia, which officially recognize several languages within their borders, clear geographic divisions among the linguistic groups help preserve political stability and a status quo among the various regions. Of course, as this book goes to press, the Yugoslav experiment is in grave danger, with several republics threatening secession. Clearly, the lack of a common tongue provides a further force contributing to this entropy —rather than aiding in political dialogue that might *prevail against* the forces tearing this fragile country apart.

There are more differences than similarities between the countries cited above and the United States. If we were to have our government operate officially in two or more languages, it would certainly be for different reasons from those discussed above.

Until recently, America has not had large enclaves of

linguistically distinct populations. Ethnic neighborhoods, yes, but not whole cities or regions where a language other than English was the main medium of communication.

And, from the earliest waves of immigrants in the 19th century to today's new arrivals, all newcomers who wish to work, study, or otherwise live productive lives in this country arrive with the expectation that they will learn English. There is no law demanding it, but experience tells us this is the most effective way to survive and enhance your prospects for success.

Stephen Baker believes, from his own experience, that this is not some abstract concept or philosophical issue. "For the immigrant, language *is* survival. You come to America with little time to philosophize and a whole lot of focus on survival. You don't sit and analyze what your position on language is going to be—you just react, on a basic level, to the need to learn the language of the people you will be dealing with on a daily basis. To be understood, or not to be understood—that is the question."

Now, however, calls for official bilingualism have become louder and clearer—particularly from some Hispanic leaders who profess to speak on behalf of Spanish-speaking people in the United States. While the threat official bilingualism poses may not seem grave today, just consider whether, 21 years ago, anyone would have predicted that the Canadian government would now be at the point of disintegrating because of language!

Bilingual education is being touted as the means for preparing the rapidly growing, non-English-speaking Hispanic population for the world of skilled work in America. However, for reasons I will go into in a later chapter, 20 years of bilingual education in this country has produced inadequate results. Not only has the dropout rate for Hispanic youth remained steady at 40% for the past decade (according to former Education Secretary Lauro Cavazos), but also indicators of earnings show that Hispanics are not rising *as a group* in economic status.

More and more research has found that the true cause of these problems is not, as many might feel, discrimination. Rather, the lack of literacy in English seems to hurt the chances of Hispanics far more than the color of their skin.

This is not just a matter of opinion. Several studies bear out this conclusion. A 1976 study conducted by the Census Bureau demonstrated a strong connection between low proficiency in English and low earnings. To determine this, the Survey of Income and Education (the official name of the study) included eight questions on spoken English usage.

Researchers from the University of California (Los Angeles) drew the following conclusion from the SIE data: "Differences associated with English language skills explain virtually all of the Hispanic wage differences usually attributed to ethnicity, national origin, and time in the United States."

The only limitation of the Census Bureau study was that it focused on *oral* English skills and did not seek to determine proficiency in *reading* and *writing*, skills that have a stronger correlation to economic achievement. But this shortcoming was soon to be corrected.

Reading proficiency in English was tested in 1985 by the National Assessment of Educational Progress, an arm of the U.S. Department of Education. Again, the results were unambiguous and unequivocal. As Rutgers economist Francisco Rivera-Batiz said, "English language proficiency can completely explain away wage differentials between immigrants and the native-born."

The implications of such a conclusion are also quite clear—and promising. The fact that the *per capita* income of Hispanics in America was so low was found to be primarily due to the heavy recent immigration of younger workers with little formal education or English proficiency. What is promising about this is that it can so easily be *corrected*: with educational opportunities, Hispanics can eliminate their economic disadvantage once and for all.

As Dinesh Desai says, "The better you speak English, the *more* opportunities you have to communicate with *more* people in a *more* precise manner." That translates to brighter prospects for a happy, prosperous life in the United States, no matter who you are or where you came from.

V.

E Pluribus Unum: A Recipe For Unity

Language enriches life, because it allows us to tell others about our experiences, our impressions, and our deeply held beliefs. As Dinesh Desai says, "I love to be able to talk to others. It is one of the greatest joys of my life, to talk about many subjects on many levels to many different people. This is so basic, yet so invaluable!"

As many immigrants who are immensely proud of their native lands would be eager to tell you, speaking English has given them a unique opportunity to share the riches of their native cultures with Americans from other backgrounds. When we can transmit our culture to others, it helps preserve the culture for posterity as well.

But immigrants from any nation who don't adapt in some form are doomed to see their cultures die off entirely as they become permanently cut off from the mainstream.

Cynthia Tam learned this in her experiences with the Chinese community in San Francisco. "Unlike the language spoken in China, the Chinese spoken in San Francisco is very antiquated. Instead of saying 'refrigerator' they say 'icebox'. They don't have a word for 'telephone'—they just call them 'ringing lines'. This Chinese is not a progressive, evolving language—it's a dying language that will die with the elderly Chinese now speaking it."

What these neighborhoods preserve is valuable and worthwhile to the people who live there. It is even enriching to other Americans. But, without some kind of contact with outsiders and other cultures, these pockets of culture often stagnate and, ultimately, perish.

Whether immigrants decide to live among their own people or strike out on their own is an individual decision. Some do better living and working among their own—others prefer to mix with Americans from different backgrounds.

But whichever option they choose, *all* of the immigrants who adapt successfully are able to do so because they've mastered the English language.

Let's take a look at a few of these "transplanted" people to see the kinds of adaptations and accomplishments they've made.

Life and Death

Vietnamese immigrant Mai Duong has been living with her family in the United States since 1975.

As a social worker with the Central Entry for Refugees in Arlington County, Virginia, since 1981, Mai helps new immigrants find work and lodging and create new lives for themselves in America. Having once been in their shoes, she knows well the immense difficulties they must face and overcome.

"Learning the English language is one of the most important things immigrants have to do when they arrive. I urge every new refugee I meet to attend ESL classes and get English under their belt as soon as possible."

When Mai first arrived in the U.S., she found a job within two weeks with the American Red Cross. She had learned

English in Vietnam and worked with Americans in programs like Foster Parents and the Save the Children Foundation. There, though, apart from her dealings with American clients, she spoke primarily Vietnamese with her supervisors, administrators, and directors.

Coming to the United States and listening to English was quite different—shockingly so! Her English teachers in Vietnam had been Vietnamese, so she did not learn from a native speaker. The accent, tone, and cadence of speech in the U.S. were too difficult to understand and follow at first.

Mai was the only one in her family who spoke *any* English when they arrived. She was the main contact with the outside world.

Mai immediately enrolled herself in English classes. Many of her co-workers at the Red Cross spoke Vietnamese, but she knew she would need English to cope with the demands of her day-to-day environment. She would watch television and read books in English to improve her skills. She made slow but steady progress.

"Even now, though, I don't think my English is good enough. I understand almost everything, but I still have problems speaking and making myself understood. I still take English privately with a tutor to improve my speaking."

Mai herself underwent professional retraining once she was in the United States, even though she came with a degree in social work. She took university courses to gain her American credentials, as well as to keep up with the latest developments in her field.

"I want to improve my English so that I can keep up with the professional literature in social work. Better English skills will make me a better professional, too."

Mai sees English as *the* critical component of the success and survival of immigrants in the United States of America, because misunderstandings—some innocent, some not-so-innocent—arise easily for those who don't learn to speak and read English.

Mai's grandmother came from Vietnam when she was 92. Mai's mother met her at the airport in New York. The grandmother had to use the bathroom, but since neither one could read, the mother ended up leading her into the *men's room*. That caused quite a commotion—and made the police sit up and take notice!

Right after that episode, Mai's mother started taking ESL classes. She eventually learned English well enough to get a job with the U.S. Department of Transportation, where she put in ten years of service prior to her retirement.

Lack of English is a particularly important problem with the Vietnamese in the Arlington area (a suburb of Washington, D.C.). Many Vietnamese live in close proximity to one another, so there's already a temptation not to learn English but to use the mother tongue exclusively.

There are other incentives as well to retaining only your mother tongue. When Mai came to the U.S., she had only to present her Vietnamese driver's license to get an American one. She thinks it is a step in the right direction that immigrants can no longer do this.

On the other hand, English is still not a requirement for passing the written test. Most of Mai's clients take the examination in Vietnamese at the Department of Motor Vehicles. Tests are offered in a variety of languages.

"I know how to drive, whether it's here or in Vietnam," says Mai. "That's not the question. But how can you read traffic *instructions* in English if you can't speak the language?"

Level of education is most definitely a stumbling block to picking up English. While the first refugees from Vietnam were well-educated, professional people, the "boat people" of the early 1980s were peasants, fishermen, and laborers who had little or no schooling in Vietnam. People who come up from the bottom have the hardest row to hoe. Many stay in the U.S. for years and years without learning English at all.

So that they might have a chance to improve their conditions, Mai tries to steer these people to the Refugee Education Employment Program (REEP), which provides English classes free to refugees. (Other immigrants pay something, usually according to their capabilities, or they are awarded grants to pay for the course.)

English-as-a-second-language classes are often held throughout the day in area Catholic churches, Buddhist temples, and YMCAs. These places usually serve as centers for refugees to congregate and have many of their basic needs addressed.

"As a refugee, you quickly realize that, if you can't speak English, people think you are stupid. Everyone knows that's not really true, and no one really says that out loud, but everyone *acts* as if the person just isn't very intelligent."

The vast majority of people Mai works with are extremely frustrated by their language limitations. Adjustments to life in the U.S. can be overwhelming, and problems with language only make the adjustments more difficult.

"Many people come to me who have been accused of shoplifting or any number of things—most of which are based on a misunderstanding. In Vietnam, a woman goes through a store and puts what she wants to buy in her bag. Then she goes to the counter to pay for it. In America, if you put things in your own bag, you're taken for a shoplifter.

"Of course, many of these people are not capable of explaining what they have done—or *not* done, as the case may be. It's really sad."

Many are in a high-pitched emotional state when they seek Mai's help.

"I have people who tell me they're thinking about committing suicide—they're *that* mad about being falsely accused and being unable to explain their innocence! That, in a nutshell, is why English is so important to these people, so they can communicate and protect their honor.

"It's truly terrible what not knowing English does to your self-esteem. Not being able to communicate in English makes you feel worthless and unable to defend yourself when you've been wrongly accused."

These people are fortunate to live in an area where someone like Mai is available to help resolve problems. Many communities do not have the funding to make such help available.

Beyond the day-to-day routine placing of immigrants in jobs and homes, giving them orientation, and telling them about English instruction in their neighborhoods, Mai does a lot of crisis management where her English skills are desperately needed.

Perhaps the most discouraging part of Mai's caseload comes from friction between refugee children and their parents. Here, too, language plays a big role in the family rifts. The children learn English in school and on the street, and they adapt to American life quickly. Then, they come home and realize their parents or grandparents don't speak English and are set in their "old ways".

On the lighter side, Mai has known Vietnamese who went into a store to buy a birthday card. Since they can't read, they pick up a pretty-looking card and pay for it, not realizing they are sending a sympathy card!

Mai once had a client who sent a birthday card to her mother that read "*from* your loving mother". The girl knew the word "mother" but didn't understand the rest of the phrase, so she wasn't aware that the card was inappropriate.

So much of the need for speaking English boils down to a question of self-expression.

"What's important for the refugee in America today? To

learn English. That's probably the most important thing they can do to adapt to life here. They need to be able to express how they feel, what they want, what they are going to do—the basic things in life!

"Emotionally, it makes all the difference in the world. There are times when I can't make myself understood even today, and it makes me depressed. My self-esteem suffers. So I can imagine what it does to people whose English is *really* limited."

Mai's personal struggle with English continues daily—and she perseveres in trying to master the subtleties and characteristic speech of American English. Over the years, her own children have been a great source of language learning. Mai exclaims, "I love learning English *with* children—whether mine or someone else's. Children speak very clearly and very slowly, so it's a good way to learn. And you're not threatened by them."

Having grown up in America and gone to the public schools, Mai's children speak English fluently and without accent. They routinely correct Mai's English usage and pronunciation—which she encourages!

She still speaks to them in Vietnamese at home. They understand Vietnamese, but they don't speak it well. Mai is not too concerned about this. She feels she has preserved the Vietnamese culture at home, but she is happy that they speak English, now that they are Americans.

"I don't want them to forget about Vietnamese culture, but I also want them to learn about American culture. *We are mixing now*, and they need to know both."

Mai is proud of her children. They are all in college and doing very well. She feels as though she must have done something right.

A Young Girl's Odyssey

Cynthia Tam was not the first in her family to come to North America. Her grandfather made the voyage before her. But it was not a direct or simple route. An opium addict in China in the 1940s, Cynthia's grandfather had squandered the family fortune. He went from being a landlord to a humble tenant farmer, all because of his costly addiction.

Then, one day when he was thrown off the streets and into a church by a group of bouncers, he had a conversion. He decided to reform his ways and try to recoup his financial losses. Since North America was touted as the place one could make a fortune with hard work, Cynthia's grandfather came to Ontario, where he set up a food concession for the itinerant railroad workers. He sent his earnings back to his family, who were able to buy back all the land they had lost because of his addiction.

But as he was returning to China by boat, his success complete, Cynthia's grandfather fell ill and died before he reached home. The dream of success in the new world lived on, however, as Cynthia's family made their way one by one to America, over a period of ten years.

Cynthia's uncle was first in the family to arrive in the U.S. A few years later, Cynthia's brother arrived on American shores, to be followed by Cynthia and her mother in 1969. Last, her father came.

Cynthia's mother was convinced that Hong Kong would eventually be overrun by the Chinese communists, so she had been preparing for a long time to get her entire family out of the country. Her daughter was a major part of the plan.

Before leaving Hong Kong, her mother had put Cynthia in a British school there, in large part so that she could learn English. While never really learning the language herself, her mother understood that to get somewhere in the world—in *any* part of the world—Cynthia would have to speak English.

In addition to the British school, Cynthia got training at home: her mother made her *memorize* 10 pages of an English text every day. All of this in preparation for their setting sail to America!

Cynthia had taken about six years of English in school before arriving in the U.S. at the age of 12, but it seemed like scant preparation for the "real thing". The British English and the academic, stilted language used in school were hardly comparable to what she would find in America.

In San Francisco, there was no one to help with the basics of life—finding a place to live, getting a job, opening accounts. It became a daily challenge for Cynthia and her mother. And 12-year-old Cynthia bore the burden of responsibility for them both.

Though at first not a very outgoing person, Cynthia was forced to become more aggressive when the Tams arrived in the States. (Her brother was not close to the rest of the family, and he was often not available to help Cynthia and her mother as they were getting settled.) Whenever there was something to translate from English into Chinese—a form, a sign, a conversation with an American—Cynthia's mother would turn to Cynthia for help.

Her mother was shy, showed little aptitude in learning English, and had little desire to pick up a new language. But for Cynthia, the opposite was true. She learned fast and was eager for every new word in her vocabulary.

Her mother would hand her forms to fill out, and Cynthia would sit down with a dictionary and decipher them. She made rapid progress in the basic vocabulary of everyday life, quickly picking up words and expressions she had never had to learn before in her more "formal" English training.

Her mother did not spend much time with other Chinese

in the Bay Area where they settled. Instead, she relied heavily on Cynthia. She even took her daughter as translator on her own job interviews and to fill out applications for her!

"Somehow, I think it's easier if you're younger. You've got a lot less to lose when you're young. And you don't think about many of the dangers of being in a city alone with all your possessions on you. The younger you are, the easier it is to handle the uncertainties of life and language."

Cynthia enrolled in school, starting in the eighth grade. But there was a problem. Her English was only at a second- or third-grade level. It took her a good nine months to pick up enough English in class before she could attempt to answer the teacher's questions.

In fact, in the first six months of school, Cynthia made it a point never to answer questions that involved *words*! In her science and math classes, if the problems involved only numbers and the solution was a number, she would confidently call out the numerical answer—but no words.

In the first years, she had to concentrate very hard whenever she spoke in English. She found, however, that tools such as speed reading helped a lot in her speaking. They gave her the ability to visualize whole sentences, whole thoughts in her head before she opened her mouth—so that when she did speak, a whole thought or sentence would then come out.

For Cynthia, learning English by watching television had strong limitations. For one, things went by so fast, you couldn't really sit there with a dictionary and look up words quickly enough. More important, it's a one-way process where you listen, but you cannot try out your own English on the characters on the screen. It was not interactive, as educators would say.

And she picked up English in some rather unusual ways as well. At age 12, she helped out her brother, who worked in a liquor store. Words like "pint", "fifth", and so on were among the first vernacular terms she learned!

While she was in school, she always maintained a part-time job outside—sometimes two jobs. This gave her a good deal of contact with English-speaking Americans from all walks of life.

Within two years in America, she was comfortable speaking English. In five years, she was confident of her abilities. After 10 years, she noticed that English was taking the place of Chinese in her daily thoughts and speech. One indication of this was her first dream in English—this was when she realized she was a fluent English speaker.

In 1974, Cynthia graduated from high school in Oakland and got a job in the engineering office of BART, the Bay Area's public transportation agency. Not long after she started, she was baited and insulted by one of her superiors, who told her that her English was hard to understand. "Where the heck did you learn how to speak and write so strangely?" he asked her mockingly.

Rather than be discouraged and insulted, Cynthia took it as a goad to show him how far she could go. Almost immediately, she enrolled at Berkeley and began an intensive major in biochemistry.

To fulfill an English requirement, she took a course that focused on Asian-American issues. She didn't know the teacher's political preferences. When Cynthia wrote a series of well-crafted, well-written papers arguing that Asians had it pretty good in America, she was shocked when she barely passed the course! The teacher didn't object to her grammar, spelling, or syntax—just her ideas!

Cynthia felt strongly, however, that oppression was much worse back home in China than it could possibly be here for the Chinese immigrants, and she made no bones about saying it. "If this were to happen to me today, I would take that teacher to court!"

When Cynthia went to college, she gave up many loves —art, music, literature—so that she could prepare for a career after school was over. As a graduate student in biotechnology, she worked a while with a professor in a laboratory. But, after several months of tiring work, literally from sunup to sunset with no human contact whatsoever, she decided to change careers.

She gave up her dream of medical school and began working with her brother in his business. It was at this time that she became acquainted with the commodities market, beginning to heat up in the late 1970s. For three years, she studied the market intensively on her own. She then got a job working on the floor of the Pacific Stock Exchange in San Francisco. Even though she was licensed and experienced, for more than a year she couldn't get a job as a retail stockbroker.

"I don't think San Francisco was ready for Chinese women stockbrokers at the time. So I moved to Washington, D.C., arriving the day after the Air Florida crash, got a job with a brokerage firm, and had to prove myself. I was fortunate in that I soon got the opportunity to be a 'line person', which showed others that I was capable and gave me tremendous experience. Again, I was able to meet a great challenge!"

Now a successful investment analyst who works out of her home *and* raises two children, Cynthia gives credit to her new land for the opportunities it offers. "American culture is essentially an open culture. People speak to one another on a first-name basis, which doesn't happen in many countries in the world. America is also open to new ideas and is flexible. That's something that many Americans don't appreciate about their own society, but believe me, once you've been to China or the East, you really value it."

VI.

Bilingual Education: Does It Work?

Much ink has been spilled and many research hours and dollars have been spent trying to decide whether bilingual education works. For 20 years now, bilingual education programs have been a fact of life in many school districts.

But "bilingual education" can encompass many different things. It is intended to be a way of getting foreign-language-speaking children to learn English *gradually* while receiving instruction in other subjects in their native language. But there has been so much dispute over the definition of "gradually" and the extent to which native-language instruction is truly valuable that we now have as many types of bilingual education programs as there are opinions on the matter.

The most prevalent form is Transitional Bilingual Education (TBE), in which students are taught subject matter (math, science, history) in their mother tongue, while they are given English instruction in increasingly large doses over a three-year period. During the first year, English instruction can be limited to as little as 45 minutes per day. Even by the third year, instruction may only be 50% in English.

TBE is endorsed because it supposedly helps the

immigrant child learn content while learning English and, at the same time, retaining his or her ethnic language and culture and identity. A large, well-entrenched bureaucracy has sprouted up to oversee these kinds of bilingual education programs. Despite the fact that these programs have gotten bad report cards, too much is at stake in the education bureaucracy for anything to change very rapidly or very substantially.

But that is precisely what ought to happen if we want immigrant children to have the same opportunities that English-speaking children now receive. Because TBE students get so little instruction in English, they fall behind their peers in the regular classrooms. When it comes time to mainstream them into classes with English-speaking students and teachers, they are most often insufficiently prepared.

Foundations like U.S.ENGLISH and individuals like the educators featured in this chapter favor a more accelerated transition into instruction in English. Support in the native language should be one of the tools teachers can use in teaching the limited-English-proficient student, to make herself or himself understood; discussion in English, however, should be encouraged as much as possible. Within a period of three years or less, the immigrant child should be mainstreamed in classes with his or her English-speaking peers.

There needs to be more flexibility of approach to deal with the varying concentrations of immigrant children. Certainly, a school district in which the only immigrants are Spanish-speaking can accommodate a TBE program more easily than one in which immigrants speak a wide variety of languages. Trying to meet the needs of the latter group through TBE would require an extensive staff of bilingual education teachers; even if the money and resources were available for this approach, it is not the most efficient alternative.

It is not my intention to jump into the fray of this very complex and technical debate. But I would like to offer the personal experiences of others as testimony to the problems of teaching immigrant children who desperately need to learn English to adjust to their new home, the United States.

Several of these individuals are teachers, who can comment on bilingual education from two perspectives, as children of immigrants and as educators.

Rosalie Porter, bilingual education expert and daughter of Italian immigrants who spoke little English when they arrived in the U.S., recalls her introduction to first grade not long after arriving in this country. "During those first few months, the hours I spent in the classroom were a haze of incomprehensible sounds. I copied what the other children seemed to be doing, scribbling on paper as though I were writing; otherwise, I silently watched the behavior of teachers and students. Although I cannot recall the process of learning English and beginning to participate in the verbal life of the classroom, I know it was painful. I can remember, however, that within two years I felt completely comfortable with English and with the school community—how it happened I do not know. . . . When it finally began to happen, I remember the intense joy of understanding and being understood, even at a simple level, by those around me."

Dr. Porter has been working in the bilingual education field in Massachusetts since the early 1970s. She most certainly doesn't advocate the kind of "sink or swim" method by which she herself learned English as a child; most often, this insensitive method of assimilating immigrant children result-ed in their dropping out of school from discouragement or confusion. This phenomenon tended to create the social underclass that education has always sought to prevent.

On the other hand, Dr. Porter's exposure to the TBE program has left her with the distinct impression of the "failures of a twenty-year national policy based on an untested learning theory that, far from helping language-minority children, actually impedes their progress." The ideas behind TBE seem logical on paper, but the results in terms of the education of immigrant children are less than satisfactory. They tend to fall behind other children not only in their English skills, but in many other subjects as well—in part because bilingual teachers often have limited credentials to teach in these subject areas.

The problem of educating non-English-speaking children is not small-scale. Language-minority children make up 10% of American schoolchildren today. In some school districts, they can constitute from 25% to 60% of the school population. It is estimated that, by the year 2000, language-minority children could make up about 20% of all children in American schools.

So how best to educate them? How do we teach them English as quickly and efficiently as possible, while not letting them slip behind their peers in other subjects? How can we make sure these youngsters get the same preparation to cope with the opportunities and changes in the world once their education is complete?

These are the questions whose answers are debated in the halls of government and the education bureaucracy, although not always with the objectivity and clear-headedness that are sorely needed. Of course, the outcome of the debates *should* determine how best to provide equal opportunities and access for *all* children.

One way of dealing with the problem of educating non-English-speaking children is to treat it as a purely practical matter, or on a case-by-case or regional basis. That was Esther Eisenhower's recommendation to the School Board—with resoundingly successful results. Dr. Eisenhower and the staff of instructional services established one of the most effective language programs for immigrants—an English-as-a-second-language curriculum—in Fairfax County, Virginia, just outside Washington, D.C.

The demographics of this area dictated against setting up a TBE-type program. Fairfax County had students who spoke 72 different languages. No school had more than two or three children of any given language group. In each classroom, you might have between four and nine language groups represented. Dr. Eisenhower knew immediately that providing bilingual education for all of these permutations would not only be extremely cumbersome and complicated—but would most likely break the school district's budget as well!

Dr. Eisenhower also found that, in addition to being multi-ethnic and multi-lingual, Fairfax County lacked a qualified force of bilingual teachers. Certainly, there were not enough to fulfill the needs of this diverse immigrant population dispersed over a wide area. (A similar problem can be found in the Los Angeles–area school districts, with a special twist: some districts import "qualified" bilingual teachers from countries such as Spain, who may speak Spanish fluently but can barely speak a word of English!)

The approach adopted for the Fairfax County ESL program was therefore flexible. Highly trained teachers were selected. They were given intensive training in teaching English as a second language. The regular curriculum was adapted to the special needs of these ESL students. The result was that the students were following as closely as possible the same curriculum presented to the regular (non-ESL) students at the same grade level. At the same time, they were learning this curriculum almost exclusively in English.

"This system worked extremely well for us," explains Dr. Eisenhower, "but, just like bilingual education, it cannot be advocated across the board. There are schools where a different system might work better, depending on the demographics of the district."

Dr. Eisenhower doesn't object to bilingual education as a concept—she just has a hard time feeling that its implementation is always handled properly.

"Bilingual education has become a highly politicized issue—almost too politicized for the good of the immigrant student. The powerful bilingual lobby will see to it that this form of education goes on, not because it's the best thing for the students, but because it ensures jobs for certain types of teachers.

"The biggest problem so far is that it perpetuates a system where some very mediocre teachers, using mediocre materials and curricula, are teaching classes and getting poor results."

During the 1980s, Dr. Eisenhower served on a blue-ribbon Department of Education panel to examine the state of bilingual education in America. She was appalled by much of what she saw and heard about. "We held hearings and visited schools across the country. It was a truly hair-raising experience for me. The only word I can find for what I saw is this—incompetence."

It seems fair to say that the debate over bilingual education needs to focus more squarely on the *goals* we are trying to achieve in educating today's immigrant children to be tomorrow's American citizens.

Although there is still so much we don't understand about how children learn, what motivates them, and what might harm them, no conclusive evidence has been offered that educating foreign-born children in English is detrimental to their self-esteem, their sense of cultural identity, or their ability to retain their mother tongue, the language spoken in their homes and neighborhoods.

In this regard, let's listen to another voice of personal experience, that of Richard Rodriguez, a Mexican-American writer, on his early experience with mastery of English:

"One day in school I raised my hand to volunteer an answer. I spoke out in a loud voice. And I did not think it remarkable when the entire class understood. That day, I moved very far from the disadvantaged child I had been only days earlier. The belief, the calming assurance that I belonged in public, had at last taken hold. . . . I [had learned] the great lesson of school, that I had a public identity."

One important conclusion that Rosalie Porter came to after years of teaching bilingual education classes, seems all too simple, yet has eluded many educators: the more time a child spends on a given task or subject, the more knowledge the child acquires about that particular subject. If English in a TBE class were taught for only 45 minutes per day, it will be reflected in the amount and quality of English spoken by the child in the class. If another TBE teacher uses more time to teach in English, those students will learn more English as well.

After several years of trying to teach her classes primarily in Spanish, Dr. Porter found it more useful to switch increasingly to English in her classroom. She found the results astonishing—and she discovered that, even when she asked her children questions in Spanish, they often preferred to answer her in English.

Cynthia Tam saw what happened to many of her compatriots from China who went through bilingual education programs. She has a strong, well-thought-out opinion on the matter:

"I think bilingual education ultimately does more harm than good. Without unification through a common language, you can only have fragmentation in a society.

"Why turn back the hands of time? In China, it took 5,000 years to get to the point where one common dialect is spoken throughout the country. Why should we turn around and do the opposite?"

In her view, bilingual education is too long and slow a process. Since it usually takes five to ten years to learn English through this teaching technique, it seems to be more of an obstacle than an opportunity to get ahead in American society. It puts the immigrant child five to ten years *behind* others.

"I could see bilingual programs that went on for half a school year or even the entire year. But it shouldn't go on forever. First things first: if you go live in a country, why not learn the language of that people? That's the simplest, most effective means to make your way in the new society."

In the long term, education policy affects the character of our democratic society. Linguistic equality—the knowledge that you can speak with and understand others around you—contributes to the goal of political and racial equality as well. The struggle for official bilingualism in America runs contrary to the civil rights movement of the past 40 years, which has sought to give *everyone*—black, brown, and white—the same opportunities and the same rights. Isn't it quite possible that strict bilingual education policies could *undo* the progress this nation has made toward equality of race, gender, and religion?

VII.

Teachers' Perspectives

Perhaps there's nowhere better to look for *accomplished* immigrants than among those who have become bilingual education teachers. They may have led difficult lives arriving in and adjusting to America, yet they are so appreciative for what they have received from this country that they're spending their careers paying back a little of this gratitude in service to the children of new immigrants.

Many of these teachers have interesting stories and their own distinct views on bilingual education. I present two of them to you:

The Long And Winding Road

Rosa Maria Rossier came to America 31 years ago, speaking no English. Today she is a successful public school teacher who has helped many immigrant school children learn English.

How did she get to where she is today?

With lots of frustration, hard work, dedication, and down-to-earth, commonsense notions of how to learn and teach the English language.

Rosa Maria's first year in the United States was much more difficult than she could have imagined. She had married her husband in Mexico City in 1959, then came almost immediately to California to live. Because she didn't have a high school education, although she had taken a few English courses, she wasn't prepared for what she found in the U.S.

All of her neighbors, in-laws, and friends spoke only English. At the time, there was no television and only two radio stations in Spanish. On her own, she was forced to pick up as much English as quickly as she could. In retrospect, she appreciates having had this opportunity, but at the time, it just made her feel extremely depressed.

"I spent the entire first year with one big, long headache!" Rosa Maria had a dictionary in every room of the house. She was always afraid the telephone would ring and she wouldn't understand what she was hearing. When her husband came home at night, he spoke to her only in English, even though she would answer him in Spanish.

Since she had not completed her high school education, she went back to night school and summer school whenever she could find the time. She spent the first two years just taking English courses before she could continue with other subjects she needed for graduation.

In the meantime, she raised three children. "I guess I was fortunate, not because we were wealthy but because everyone was so understanding and helpful to me. I never once had to get a babysitter or leave my children alone because, when I was studying at night, my husband would be with them."

As her children grew up, Rosa Maria was very involved in *their* schooling as well. She was a room mother actively involved in whatever ways she might be needed. These experiences gave her a taste for teaching that increased with the years.

By the time the last child went to college, Rosa Maria had her Bachelor's degree in child development, plus a multiple subject credential and special education credentials needed for teaching. She was interested in working with the deaf, and her first job was as an instructional aide in special education.

While working as an instructional aide in the deaf education program, she was approached by a district administrator who was impressed with her facility in English and Spanish. He urged her to go into bilingual education, saying the district would pay her way through school. Rosa Maria refused, however, for three reasons: (1) she didn't want to be *obligated* to teach a specific subject, (2) she wanted to continue teaching deaf children, and (3) she didn't put much faith in bilingual education. She saw her sister's children having trouble in the bilingual classes they were attending, and she wasn't sure this was the way to go.

The story of how she went from a substitute teacher to a bilingual, full-time teacher is a story of courage and strong conviction. Rosa Maria had taken over a combined first and second grade class of 33 children, most of them Chinese. She was being considered for the job full-time. But when she was approached by the school administration and asked to sign a bilingual waiver, mandating that she learn Chinese and use it in her classroom, she resolutely refused.

(Permit me to interject a brief explanation in Rosa Maria's story. A "bilingual waiver", in my opinion, is one of the ugly facts of bilingual education. A teacher who is urged to sign this waiver must learn a foreign language and be able to teach in it within five years, *or he or she loses the job*! And gaining mastery of the language is no mean feat—you must do it on your own time and with your own money, while carrying a full-time load of classes. Small wonder that many people see these waivers as one reason why many good teachers are leaving the school system!)

At the parent-teacher conference held at the end of the first grading period, it became apparent that Rosa Maria was overwhelmingly popular with both parents and students. Her effectiveness paid off, and she was asked to stay in a regular classroom.

When she began teaching, she found children of all nationalities in her classroom, particularly those from Central and South America and from Vietnam. A most disturbing trend became apparent to her: whenever she acquired new students from the bilingual education program, she noticed how deficient they were in almost *all* skills. In her third grade class, she would get children who didn't yet know the alphabet and couldn't read or write at all.

Since 1983, she has taught at Garfield Elementary School in a bilingual classroom. She has developed her own instructional approach, based not only on her experience teaching immigrant students, but also on her personal experience in learning English.

"The only way for these children to become bilingual is for them to learn English in school. They're learning the basics of their mother tongue at home, and many of them will have the opportunity later to learn the formal aspects of their native language in foreign language classes. In the meantime, though, what they need most is English."

All her instructional materials (reading and math books) are in English. She has a bilingual aide in the class (a requirement of bilingual programs) and she does teach *some* Spanish songs, dances, and poems (some of which she also teaches in sign language!), but for the most part everything is done in English.

At parent-teacher meetings, parents often plead with Rosa Maria *not* to instruct their children in Spanish. They want to make sure their children learn English properly, so they will have the same chances the other kids have.

Rosa Maria agrees to do it their way, because she believes they are right. She also encourages them to continue teaching their children Spanish at home. "I want these children to be proud of their backgrounds, just as I am of mine. Even in the classroom, I like to get them to talk about their cultures and traditions."

Every year, Rosa Maria puts on an elaborate Cinco de Mayo celebration in which she likes to get everyone— parents and children—involved. She gets the parents to bring in foods and articles peculiar to their countries of origin; she has the children present songs, plays, and poems from their homelands; she organizes displays of the costumes and customs of different countries. And, as much as possible, she has them do it in English—so that everyone can understand and appreciate these traditions.

"Exposing these children to different cultures only enriches their appreciation for their own cultures. The only constant has to be language—or we cannot communicate cultural traditions to one another."

In 1987, Rosa Maria was chosen as one of three elementary school teachers to serve on Governor Deukmejian's California Commission on Educational Quality. She was exposed to many different classrooms and teaching styles, attended numerous hearings, and helped write recommendations to the governor. These experiences served to solidify her feelings about bilingual education, too. "I never felt stronger that English had to be taught as much as possible in every classroom. It helps dissolve discrimination and foster love and understanding among students. This is perhaps the most valuable lesson we can teach them."

Because of her commitment to and excellence in teaching, she was also one of five California teachers to be invited to President George Bush's inauguration. She felt this was the highest honor and privilege of her life.

Despite the fact that she became an American citizen as soon as she could, Rosa Maria still feels attached to her homeland. She is proud of her Mexican roots, but she is equally proud of the United States and the opportunities it makes available to all its citizens.

Rosa Maria feels that life in this country has given her more than she has been able to return. "If they didn't pay me a dollar, I would still teach. I do it for one simple reason: many people helped me when I first came here, and now it's my turn to help others. I can't tell you how grateful I am to the United States of America and its wonderful people!"

Swimming To Shore

Language and living are so intertwined in the experience of the immigrant—it's hard to separate them or consider them apart from one another.

Rosalie Porter was the oldest of five children of Italian parents. The family left their small Italian village to come to the United States in 1936. But they didn't all come over at the same time, and that was a big heartbreak to the young Rosalie.

Her mother was already an American citizen, who came over in early 1936 by herself. The family's move to this country was motivated by the increasing instability in Italy and the prospects of war. Rosalie's father and the eldest three children (the youngest two were not yet born) remained in Italy for another year before reuniting with their mother. That was a painful year for the kids, who missed their mother terribly.

"I was six when I arrived in Newark, New Jersey. I spoke no English — and my parents didn't either! Needless to say, the first months were confusing in the extreme, in fact quite frustrating."

92

On Rosalie's first day of school, her parents took her to the local grade school and left her there. She hardly knew why she was there. At the end of a mystifying first day, the children were dismissed from class and led out a different door from the one they went in. Rosalie had *no idea how to get home*! She wandered for miles in Newark until a kind policeman spotted her and tried to help, sensing she was lost.

Of course, *he* spoke no Italian, so he took Rosalie to the nearest Italian grocery store, where the owner could translate for them and the policeman could guide her to her doorstep.

"That was how I felt during the first months in America —lost! And there was no special help given to me in the classroom, either."

The saving grace was that time seemed to pass quickly. Within about a year and a half or two years, Rosalie felt quite comfortable in an American classroom, learning, speaking, reading, and writing in English.

Even today, rapid-fire acquisition of English is not uncommon, although it is more often voluntary. Rosalie tells an interesting anecdote about a young Chinese girl who recently entered the Newton, Massachusetts, school system.

When this six-year-old arrived in the U.S. (having been put on a plane by her grandmother back in Beijing), she spoke not a word of English. Her parents enrolled her in first grade and, despite being offered a bilingual program in Chinese and English, chose to place her in the regular classroom with some special help in English.

Two short years later, this little girl won a literary competition that led to the publishing of her first short story in English! A publisher held a national competition for third graders, and her teacher encouraged her to enter. Her story— "My First American Friend"—won first prize and was published in 1990. Not bad for two years of English!

Growing up in an Italian immigrant neighborhood in

Orange, New Jersey, in the 1940s had its advantages and drawbacks. It fulfilled some of her parents' dream that their children be raised as if they were back home in Italy.

It wasn't until she was in her early twenties and made her first trip back to Europe and Italy that she understood the power of her background and heritage. She had retained fluency in Italian as a teenager and young adult, but she had more or less ignored its importance in her life. She now regained some balance in her conception of who she was and where she had come from. In her own words: "I now felt proud to be *both* an American and an Italian."

Reflecting on her background, Rosalie feels it is unfortunate that immigrant children in those days were not treated with the respect they should have been given. It was in many ways a painful experience for her, feeling constantly ashamed and embarrassed about her language limitations. On the other hand, the fact that it made her learn English quickly and effectively was certainly beneficial.

"I wouldn't want today's immigrant children to go through the pain I did, so I don't recommend the methods used with me. However, I disagree with those who feel we should teach them primarily in their native language for long periods of time. They need to assimilate—perhaps more gradually than I did—but certainly over the shortest possible time."

Rosalie went on to have a successful career in high school. She came close to leaving school, but her mother intervened in time. "My parents were not sophisticated people; neither of them had more than an elementary school education. They were from a relatively poor village in Italy. So when I was old enough, my father wanted to put me to work to help support the family."

Times were tough then for Rosalie's family and, being the oldest child, she was called upon to help. Her mother, however, fought to keep her in school until she graduated from high school. "I'm forever thankful to her for prevailing over my father!"

At 17, then, Rosalie entered the world of work. For the next ten years, she worked as a file clerk, a legal secretary, and in numerous other positions, until she landed a job in an advertising agency, where she began to have something of a career in the modern sense of the word. While in the New York agency, she took night classes at Rutgers University toward a college degree.

For most of these years, Rosalie routinely sent most of her paycheck home to help her parents and her four siblings. At the end of ten years, when she married and began to raise her own family, she had two full years of college credits.

For the next 10–12 years, she was busy raising her children. In the early 1970s, with the emerging feminist movement and other "consciousness-raising" groups, she got the bug to go back to school to complete her college degree. She began teaching and was soon involved in a bilingual education program, since she had learned Spanish in school and was fluent in it.

"My years of experience with bilingual education have shown me that an ideological commitment to teaching in the native language does not always lead to the promotion of the best educational approach." She does not advocate "sink or swim" programs. She thinks we need diversity and flexibility in our approach to teaching English alongside a native language.

"We should never lose sight of the ultimate goal: to teach these children to speak, read, and write English so they can advance in American society," Rosalie says. "It's deceptive to think that you can come to this country, mix only with your own people in your native language, and do well here. You can certainly *manage* to live here and earn a decent living, but you won't be able to move out of your neighborhood—and you'll miss out on all of the opportunities to move up in position, income, and status."

The tradeoffs involved in learning English and maintaining your cultural and linguistic heritage need to be better understood and discussed, because they are not obvious. For example, it seems incompatible to maintain cultural pluralism while extending the possibility of upward mobility for all. On some fronts, these initiatives *are* incompatible, yet if cultural pluralism is set against the backdrop of a common language in which different cultures can be shared, harmony may prevail.

Even Rosalie's parents learned English eventually. They ran a local grocery store catering to Italian tastes in the Italian neighborhood. They had to learn English to be able to write checks, figure out their taxes, and so on. Eventually, it became important for them to be able to listen to the radio, watch television, and read the newspaper to know what was going on in the rest of the world, too.

According to Rosalie, "It is one of the greatest of the American freedoms that we can be as ethnic or non-ethnic as we please. Multi-culturalism has been with us for a long time in the United States—it's not something new."

There is no reason that ethnic and cultural diversity cannot exist, *so long as there are common links that bind us all.* Just as we share the common laws we live under, it's important that we also share the same means of communication.

Rosalie believes there is a tacit understanding that a common language already exists in the United States. "When you talk to people about the 'language problem' in the U.S. and the need for a common or official language, they are generally amused at your efforts, because they take it for granted that the problem could not exist. And yet it does—and it will get much worse if it is not addressed."

The promise of America has not diminished in recent years, despite appearances to the contrary. There are still opportunities for new immigrants. With hard work, education, and the right spirit, the opportunity is there for anyone to achieve anything in the U.S.

And, for those already in this country, the contribution that immigrants make is clear from history. Many great inventions, enterprises, and cultural gifts have come from immigrants who have become American citizens.

Some things have changed, however. Today's immigrants need special help learning English that wasn't given or available to immigrants in past generations. When Rosalie's family came over, there were many opportunities for unskilled workers who spoke little or no English. For example, her mother got a job almost immediately, sewing uniforms for the soldiers in World War II.

But these kinds of unskilled jobs are generally no longer available—or they're not lucrative enough to support a family! American society has evolved into a technological one, and even the jobs at the lower end of the economic spectrum are now primarily service-sector jobs where English literacy is a *must*.

In particular, immigrants from poorer, less developed countries need special language instruction in order that they might become productive citizens in our society. Today's immigrant to the United States will have a vastly increased chance of achieving happiness and prosperity if he or she sets out—and is given the opportunity—to master the English language.

* * * * *

I agree with Rosalie's assessment of bilingual education. Learning English must be the highest priority for all immigrant children. It is with this in mind that we developed Cambria Institute's Mission Statement:

"To provide the highest quality of English language instruction possible to enable non-native speakers of English to acquire a level of competency in English which makes it possible for them to join in the mainstream of American society, be it just for daily acquisition, business, or higher education."

VIII.

What's All The Fuss?

My own experiences in this country have shown me we're at a desperate crossroads. Many ethnic leaders, who by no means represent the people they claim to speak for on all subjects, have vigorously promoted bilingual initiatives that are setting back the progress of civil rights by decades. (Some Latino ethnic leaders, for example, insist that they speak on behalf of *all* Hispanics. In the process, however, they are masking the incredible diversity among Hispanics, who come from 22 different countries, speak as many or more dialects or variants of Spanish, and are part of numerous different classes and races. So, to speak on behalf of all these people is truly a large-scale task. Just the scope of this job makes you suspect the quality of their "representation" may not be very high.)

Even more disturbing are the halfhearted efforts to teach English well to the new immigrant. Throughout this book, you've heard people report on the lack of resources for learning the English language properly. The *desire* and *motivation* to learn were there—but often the appropriate instruction wasn't.

Why haven't we, as a nation, made a concerted, continuous, and sincere effort to teach English to all new inhabitants?

Our government gives away billions of dollars in welfare each year. Why can't it invest some of that money in teaching immigrants English? It would certainly improve the quality of life for many new immigrants, and it would be a true, tangible investment that would pay off for American society and the economy.

In the meantime, however, language and literacy conditions in this country are only getting worse—even if they seem to be staying the same.

Just when I felt there was a ray of hope—when the 1986 Amnesty Program promised to help new immigrants learn English in schools and community-based organizations—my hopes were dashed by the bickering and political squabbling that watered down any real benefits to the program. The resulting requirement, 40 hours of instruction in English, is horribly insufficient. It's insulting to the new immigrant—worse yet, it's like sentencing him or her to "third-class citizenship".

Yet certain very vocal lobbying organizations, purporting to speak for *all* Hispanics, or Southeast Asians, or some other immigrant group, have pushed for inadequate English instruction for adults, cumbersome and ghettoizing forms of bilingual education for our children, and firmly required multilingualism for our governments.

Let me cite a few examples of misguided opinion and wrong-headed objectives:

• Jose Moreno of the Trinity Coalition has stated that "the English plus movement promotes the use of a second language in government."

• In Chicago, City Hall now employs civil servants who are conversant in a total of 87 languages. In the words of the mayor's press secretary, "You have to offer services in more than one language. We have a lot of things to offer. The best way to make sure everyone knows about them is in another tongue besides English."

• Hispanic leaders are jubilant over the fact that bilingual education often results in children not learning any English at all. "Let's face it. We are not going to be a totally English-speaking country any more," said Aurora Helton of the Governor of Oklahoma's Hispanic Advisory Committee. And Mario Obledo, president of the League of United Latin American Citizens (LULAC), proclaims that "Spanish should be included in commercials shown throughout America. Every American child ought to be taught both English and Spanish." Interestingly, LULAC was founded more than 50 years ago to help Hispanics learn English and enter the American mainstream.

• A mayor of Miami, Florida, Maurice Ferre, sees nothing critical in having one language of government. "Citizenship is what makes us all American. Language is not necessary to the system. Nowhere does the Constitution say that English is our language."

Why would anyone in his right mind fight to institute such exclusionary policies? The claim *they* make is to preserve culture: apparently, these leaders believe immigrants are not able to learn a second language and still preserve their own birthright, their unique cultural heritage.

They say there's no reason every language group can't be accommodated—and that printing federal government signs, forms, manuals, and the like in nearly 150 languages is no big deal.

They say asking an immigrant to learn English is asking too much. Yet generations of immigrants have gladly made this investment in a new life, and many are doing so today as well.

The arguments of those who support multi-lingualism sound absurd to most immigrants who have learned English.

Even those who have not mastered English want their children to learn it. But, because of the radical anti-English groups and their pressure tactics—tactics that imply that the official-English stance is somehow racist and discriminatory —many children cannot get the English instruction they need at school!

Many advocates of a bilingual society believe the goal of bilingual education should not be to teach English at all— but primarily as a means to empower minority students. Jim Lyons of the National Association for Bilingual Education feels that "mainstreaming children is unfair, hypocritical, and racist." The real pity of outlandish statements such as this is how many people, out of a desire to uphold cultural or ethnic values, believe these statements are true!

In 1974, the U.S. Supreme Court responded to a suit brought by a Chinese family in San Francisco. They complained that their children were being denied equal educational opportunity because of the language barrier. The Court ruled that schools must give some special assistance to children who lack proficiency in English.

With the perversion of that ruling, it has been downhill all the way for immigrant children, who are often subjected to long-term, native-language-based instruction. In other words, they are taught *all* their subjects in their native language—often for years at a time!—rather than learning English quickly and intensively, so that they may become a part of the regular student body.

This may be the first generation of immigrants to America who do not see their children prosper and benefit fully from the American way of life—thanks to the wrong-headed "leaders" who say English-language instruction is too hard for immigrants!

It's important to note that these so-called leaders have some valuable territory to protect: political turf, representing millions of votes and thus enormous influence and power, *and* financial turf. Consider that the bilingual education bureaucracy has swollen into a multi-million-dollar "industry", and you'll understand why it's in the best interest of many bureaucrats *not* to teach children English in a quick, effective manner! Other government spending programs, aimed at helping impoverished immigrants who remain economically stuck because they don't know English, are also valuable turf for some ethnic leaders.

So, to the question, "why provide government services in languages other than English?", there's a very simple answer: "politics". Chicago Alderman Luis Gutierrez, speaking about the fact that City Hall can deal with problems in 87 different languages, commented that "it was a campaign promise Daley made, and I see him doing the right thing. . . . They reached out for votes in Spanish during the elections. And if you use Spanish to get the votes, you should use Spanish to provide city services."

Rabble-rousing ethnic leaders are quick to cry "foul" and "discrimination" at every opportunity. They insult the very people they claim to represent, by assuming these individuals can't cope with the task of learning English as past generations have done. And they use the preservation of ethnicity as a rallying cry that could ultimately divide our country! Martha Jimenez of MALDEF has said that "seeking communication through a common language reveals a fundamental misunderstanding of the history of language diversity in the United States, and the historical use of English in the United States as a tool of oppression."

Already, in some states, a second (and sometimes third!) language is in use by governments trying to accommodate the wishes of the anti-English "fringe" faction.

Already we see dividing lines being drawn between English-speaking Americans and those who have yet to adopt it.

Already, we can see ourselves heading for a rift in our union, as we see today in Canada.

With the other enormous challenges facing our nation—economic, environmental, and political—we cannot afford to lose the one thing that allows us to function as a strong representative democracy: *our common language.*

Fortunately, a majority of Americans—including many immigrants—support this idea wholeheartedly, as shown by a 1991 Gallup survey commissioned by U.S.ENGLISH. When 995 registered voters were asked whether they would favor or oppose making English the official language of government in the United States, 78% were in favor. These came from a strong cross section of Republicans, Democrats, Independents—and the whole political spectrum from liberal to moderate to conservative. In addition, 74% of those whose families spoke a native language other than English were in favor of official English.

The poll also revealed that only a small minority believe making English the official language of government would discriminate unjustly against anyone. Ninety-five percent felt official English was *not* discriminatory; this includes 88% of all families with a native language other than English!

The broad, strong support for official English, coupled with the leadership from this fine organization, have made it possible for certain battles to be won and others to be fought as you read this book:

• Eighteen states have passed laws declaring English to be their official language.

• Sixteen others have introduced similar legislation in their state houses.

• On the federal level, U.S.ENGLISH has spearheaded the introduction into the House and Senate of the Language of Government Act (which stipulates that the official language for government business is English) and the English Language Amendment (ELA) to our Constitution.

If passed, the ELA will at last safeguard English as the common language in the United States of America *by law*, preserving the tie that binds us and makes our government work.

Do we really need these laws? You tell me:

People are seriously advocating that every student in the United States should have the right to instruction in his or her native language.

In some areas, state and local government workers are not required to be fluent in English—so you could call to iron out a problem with your personal property tax and find yourself unable to get even the most basic information delivered to you in English. In some instances, employees are *encouraged* to speak their native languages. For example, in Arizona, a U.S. District Court judge upheld a ruling in favor of a state employee who wanted to use Spanish on the job. The judge took the occasion to declare Arizona's Official English law unconstitutional as well. (Arizonans for Official English is hoping to win the opportunity to argue against this flawed decision in the near future.)

Because of their poor command of English, millions of young men and women are leaving high school with pros- pects no brighter than a dishwasher's job at a local restaurant. Meanwhile, employers go begging for well-educated workers who can handle the high-tech jobs that have increasingly replaced blue-collar positions. What will happen to this generation, set apart socially and financially from the mainstream?

Our government has to take a stand on language and establish a clear-cut policy. It must act as a leader and proclaim loudly that English is important for survival and opportunity. Otherwise, our nation will see continued erosion of our common language and the unity of our people. Making English the official language of the United States is the first step toward establishing opportunities for immigrants to learn English.

IX.

Lessons From Those Who Came Before

No less than the leaders of two of the greatest nations on earth—the United States and the Soviet Union—have stressed the importance of learning English in the United States of America, both for the welfare of the immigrant as well as the benefit of our nation as a whole. It was President Theodore Roosevelt who said, "We have room for but one language here, and that is the English language, for we intend to see that the crucible turns our people out as Americans. No more hyphenated Americans!"

Tough realist that he was, President Roosevelt understood the necessity of speaking a common language, for the benefit of the individual and society as a whole. He realized that the individual vastly improved his chances of success in the U.S. if he mastered English, the language in common currency.

Similarly, U.S.S.R. President Mikhail Gorbachev observed the following about immigrants to our country: "Though representatives from many ethnic groups came together in the United States, English became their common language. Apparently, this was a natural choice. One can imagine what would have happened if members of each nation moving to the United States had spoken only their own tongues and refused to learn English."

Many who paved a way for themselves, who flourished in their professional and private lives, recognized the value of learning English when they came to this country. English opened up avenues and opportunities many never dreamed of before.

Naturally, success can be measured in many different ways, but I think you'll find the two case histories below to be shining examples of determination and a willingness to persevere to achieve one's aspirations.

Frontier Spirits In A Harsh World

Although Bob and Rachel Carriedo were both born in the U.S., they lived for a long time like immigrants.

Bob was born in the U.S. to Mexican parents, but his family returned to Mexico when he was only six months old. Until he came to the U.S. permanently in 1946, Bob had stayed in this country only briefly.

When Bob was nine, he came to stay with his sister in what was then called Canaryville, a mostly English-speaking neighborhood on the southwest side of Chicago (near the stockyards). His sister had children about his age, from whom he learned his first words of English.

He went to grammar school in Chicago for a year but spent most of the time at the back of the class trying to decipher what was being said. He got no special help or attention from the teachers. Somehow, between classes and his sister's children, he managed to pick up a basic grounding in English.

Bob returned to Mexico, attended school for two more years (fourth and fifth grades), and then was forced to quit school and work to help his family keep their heads above water. His family was poor, and Bob always felt an obligation to help out in whatever way he could.

"I wish it had been otherwise, but there was never enough time to go to school after those first years. I was always too busy looking after the needs of my parents. Don't get me wrong, I didn't mind it—I just never had time for formal schooling."

So that he might make better money that would go farther in helping his family, Bob came to the U.S. when he was 17.

He arrived in Chicago on the fourth of July in 1946 and landed a job the next day! (Of course, in the years after World War II, it was relatively easy to find work.)

Bob started work as an assembler with Chicago Springs, a mattress-making firm, where 60% of the workers on the line were Mexican-Americans who spoke Spanish with one another. In his first year as an adult in the U.S., Bob learned the basics of holding a conversation—small talk and shop talk—but he couldn't have written a letter or a report for work if he had to.

Bob had a tireless curiosity and desire to learn. From the outset, Bob figured that if he was going to be living and working here in the United States, he had to have a command of the English language. Whenever he heard a word that he didn't know, he'd look it up in the dictionary. That would lead him to look at the words around the one he was seeking, and he'd look at definitions, spellings, pronunciations in an effort to improve his language skills.

Another compelling reason to master English was that Bob wanted to learn more about his occupation, advance himself, and make more money so that he could offer more support to his family in Mexico.

When his father died in 1951, Bob felt a filial obligation

to help support his mother; he sent her money on a regular basis until her death in 1978.

And, even before he had come to America, Bob had actively helped his younger brother become a doctor. Bob sent money regularly to pay his brother's way through college and medical school. (Even after Bob married and had a sizable family of his own to support, his wife *insisted* that he continue sending his brother money for his studies!)

"I think it's the best investment I ever made," says Bob in a reflective tone. "My brother is now a prominent physician in Mexico. I'm very proud to have him as my brother—and I'm happy I was able to help him along in his career."

Bob's career didn't suffer, either. His natural energy and curiosity led him to move up quickly in the company. As a maintenance mechanic, Bob was constantly tinkering with the machinery to get it to perform. In the process, he devised a simple gadget to make the machinery work more efficiently. This made Bob's supervisors sit up and take notice. Bob was given more and more responsibilities and more opportunities to learn about the various machines in the factory.

Bob's rise to the top was not straight or simple. With a wife and six children to feed, clothe, and house, Bob had immediate needs far surpassing what he could earn as a maintenance engineer. He started looking around for another, more lucrative career path.

When his supervisors at the factory got wind of Bob's ambitions, they began offering him better positions to keep him in the company. They persuaded him to stay on, with opportunities to learn more about the business, to handle work crews, and to supervise operations. At this point, Bob knew he had to solidify his language skills by learning how to write idiomatic English and get his points across in letters and reports to upper management.

While his Spanish was very useful in dealing with the many Hispanic workers, his English was critical in dealing with upper management. In 1968, he was elected the local president of his union, where he gained wide recognition and visibility.

Bob later found himself in the ranks of management, first with Chicago Springs, then as a vice president and president with Simmons, which had purchased Chicago Springs. From this point forward, he spent almost two decades at the top of his business.

Although he retired several years ago, Bob is still as active as ever. His ideas have mushroomed into several successful business partnerships: a mattress-wire service and distributor, a Midwest distributor for an East Coast brush company, and two restaurants in the Chicago area.

You would never know that Bob's *formal* education was limited; his knowledge of the ways of the world and its people bespeak a man who has a Ph.D. in life experiences. He's modest to a fault, but he has a lot to be proud of!

"I have no real regrets. Life has been hard for me and my family, but we've done well, too. I only wish there had been time for me to get a full-time education."

Even though Bob may not have been able to take advantage of many educational opportunities, he made sure his children would have every chance to excel—and so they did! Among their successful offspring, Bob and Rachel count one graduate of the Naval Academy in Annapolis and one from the Air Force Academy.

If Bob and Rachel were boasters, which they most emphatically are *not*, they could rattle off reams of awards, kudos, and commendations they and their children have received for service to their schools, companies, and their country, the United States of America.

* * * * *

His wife Rachel's early years were at least as hard as Bob's. Although Rachel was born in the United States, her mother had come from a small Mexican village of only five or six homes. The family was dirt poor, and her parents never learned English. The eight children communicated with their parents in Spanish and with one another in English.

Her oldest sister gave up many opportunities on behalf of the children. This sister's sense of responsibility to her family could not have run deeper. She made a solemn vow to the other children that they would all receive their high school diplomas—a vow that was completely fulfilled.

Among other successful siblings is Rachel's brother. He won a scholarship to the University of Chicago and is now a noted psychologist. She herself, in addition to raising six children, has had an important career as a bilingual teacher's aide.

Rachel resumed work with the Chicago Board of Education in 1977, when her youngest went off to high school. Because she had done a lot of volunteer work in her children's schools and because she was fluent in Spanish, she was given a job as a bilingual aide, working with elementary school children who spoke little or no English. (Aides work closely with bilingual education teachers in developing curricula for these children and making sure that each one gets the instruction he or she needs, depending upon their language abilities and grade level in other subjects.)

In the classroom, Rachel speaks first in Spanish, then she translates and explains the English equivalents of her Spanish words. Depending upon the programs and schools she has worked in, she can be teaching a wide variety of subjects in Spanish, while the bilingual teacher mirrors the subject-matter in English. (The characteristics of the program vary with the bilingual population in a given area and with the funding level for each school.)

"I also enjoy working with the parents of these children, the new immigrants. They remind me of my parents—and I feel I have a good idea of the hardships and problems they face. It's interesting that even many younger parents from Latin countries think it's too late for them to learn English by the time they get here. They feel that Spanish is all around them in their neighborhood, their friends, often their work. Frankly, they're also a bit uncomfortable or ashamed when they try to speak, so they just don't really learn the language correctly.

"I try to help them get over this emotional block, but it doesn't always work. Clearly, though, their children will have a better chance, once they've learned the language of their new land."

Bob and Rachel obviously care about their brothers and sisters from Mexico. That's why they want to see them learn English when they come to the United States—so they can have equal access to the best opportunities this nation has to offer its hard-working inhabitants.

And, without a doubt, Bob and Rachel have been—and continue in their retirement years to be—dedicated, firmly grounded American citizens!

A Dream Come True—In Living Video

Yilmaz Turker came to the United States of America 27 years ago, with just a suitcase full of clothes. His best friend, Erol Onaran, had come two and a half years earlier, with $16 in his pocket. Erol had been trying to get Yilmaz to visit him since he had arrived in this country.

Today, Erol runs the second largest video rental operation in the Washington, D.C., area with the help of his long-time friend, Yilmaz.

Yilmaz knew almost no English, just the few words he

remembered from grammar school! When he came here, he spoke no daily, conversational English, nor did he know the language of his future business—repairing electronic items (TVs, radios).

Erol had come to the United States speaking better English, although he, too, had an adjustment period in trying to learn idiomatic, day-to-day language. Erol had studied English in high school and came to this country to complete his education. While in school, he had worked in various repair shops in the Washington area to support himself.

In many ways, Yilmaz was lucky because Erol had paved the way for him. Erol could help him get on his feet in this country and show him the ropes. While Yilmaz was adjusting to life in the U.S., the two lived together, ate together, commuted and worked together. Erol got him a job at the same hi-fi and television repair company where he worked. When Erol wasn't there, Yilmaz floundered. The first six months were very difficult, trying to communicate with others.

Yilmaz learned to speak broken English, but his bosses spoke no Turkish. Erol would act as his translator through those first difficult times.

Yilmaz acquired a good bit of English by leaving the radio on all day—while he worked, then at home at night. He would listen to news, commercials, and talk shows, trying to pick up what people were saying, how they pronounced words, what words they used.

Then he would try to apply what he'd heard in his life and work. By this informal, incessant method, he finally acquired the basics of his new language.

"It got better every day, but it was still slow. I think learning a language really depends on your personality, your desire, [your] willingness, and so on."

Once the two had settled into the repair business in the

United States, it was too late to go back to Turkey. They had talked about it and had visited their homeland—but both felt that it was too late to go back and start over.

"The first year in America was so hard that once I had that behind me and life started getting better, I had a new life in America. Things had gotten much nicer, so why should I have gone back to Turkey to start all over?"

Of course, Yilmaz did have his share of misunderstandings and mishaps in his early days in this country. One day, Yilmaz got a telephone call from a government agency to come and repair some hi-fi equipment. Yilmaz tried to get the name and address of the agency, but what he heard and wrote down was "Feller Trad Commission". He proceeded downtown and, when he couldn't find the building, he showed the piece of paper to passersby, none of whom seemed to know where this was.

Finally, in desperation he asked a man outright (without showing the piece of paper). The man pointed to the sign behind Yilmaz, which read "Federal Trade Commission," and said "You're here—it's this building here!"

Six months after Yilmaz arrived in the United States, he and Erol decided to open their own repair shop in 1963, manned by just the two of them. Yilmaz recalls how it would fill him with terror every time Erol left to make a house call.

"I would sit there hoping the telephone would ring, but also praying that it wouldn't, too. I was dying! I hoped no one would call, because I might not be able to understand them. If someone called, I just had no idea how I would communicate with them! And here we were sending out advertising to tell them to give us a call!"

The two had launched an aggressive, low-budget marketing campaign, writing up promotional cards and slipping them under the doors of neighboring houses, and talking to area merchants and department stores who sold equipment to cut deals with them for repair work. Yilmaz knew that if people called, they would expect to speak to someone in English.

Even with Erol's knowledge of electronics and Yilmaz's willingness to work hard and make a success of the business, their first year and a half brought them very little business. Things looked bleak until they moved to the suburb of Arlington, Virginia, where the neighborhood was more receptive to them and their business turned around. (By contrast, in their first shop things had gotten so bad that they had resorted to asking at the other shops to push business their way. In a way, this was easier, because the language problem was less important with referrals.)

From their Arlington shop, the two built up the business into a small empire. Always on the cutting edge of technology and popular demand for new items, they specialized first in repairing European electronics equipment—German stereos, Dutch radios, tape recorders, etc.—which few people really knew how to repair.

In 1968, they started *selling* televisions and other electronic equipment. More stores were opened, serving a broader clientele.

With nine stores in the area selling and servicing equipment, they reached an important marketing crossroads. Videocassettes became "hot" in the late 1970s, and Erol and Yilmaz began selling videos and VCRs in 1978. They were also among the first to *rent* videos in 1981. This business took off so fast and so well that within five years they had 100 "Erol's" stores.

"It was the right business at the right time," Yilmaz reflects today. "And we seemed to know what to go into. We always outstripped our competitors because we had an idea of what would be hot in the future."

Erol and Yilmaz have never forgotten how far they have

come and what they had to contend with in their early days. Perhaps that is why, for many years, they ran in-house language courses for employees at Erol's who needed to improve their English. Classes were given at three levels of proficiency and were free (and optional) to employees.

The program was instituted around the time of the end of the Vietnam war. Many Vietnamese were resettling in the Arlington area; a number of them worked for Erol's. It was Erol's and Yilmaz's intent to help them adjust as easily as possible to life and work in the United States.

At one time, when they had 600 people in the main headquarters, some 30-40 were immigrants. They were having a hard time either with bosses, co-workers, or people under them—and that's the primary reason Erol's decided to offer this type of instruction.

"It was helpful to a lot of people. These were employees at many different levels of management. Even I went to a couple of refresher classes . . . after 20 years! I still think it helps."

This informal program saw about 100-150 people pass through its doors. Many of these workers were able to advance their careers and make a more positive contribution to the company.

The instructor focused on the words, phrases, and commands workers would need in their work environments. If they were involved in purchasing, they would get instruction in the buying terminology and so forth.

"In my life, knowing English has been immensely important," Yilmaz says. "You can use English all around the world—there's always someone who speaks English wherever you go."

Yilmaz Turker can't imagine why anyone would oppose making English our nation's official language. And he has proved himself to be committed to providing high-quality English-language instruction to immigrants. He is one more successful immigrant to the United States who stands foursquare in favor of the aims of U.S.ENGLISH.

X.

U.S.ENGLISH: A Closer Look

As the United States moves into the post-industrial era, more and more of the available jobs in this country will not only require more extensive skills than ever before, but will also depend upon higher levels of language proficiency. It is estimated that, by the year 2000, three-quarters of the jobs in the United States will require education levels beyond the twelfth grade.

The immigrants of previous generations could come and earn a living as day laborers, factory workers, and various other unskilled jobs. Today, however, many of these jobs have become increasingly scarce in our changing economy.

In place of these jobs at the lower end of the spectrum, more service-oriented positions have been created for which the new, relatively unskilled immigrant might be ideally suited—provided he or she can speak English. This service sector will increase in size into the 21st century; in addition, more specialized, technically based professions will continue to draw from a base of highly trained, well-educated men and women who are literate in English.

As it is now, about 80% of the information stored in the world's computers is in English. It is also an established fact that English is the international language of aviation, navigation, technology, science, and business.

But what does this have to do with making English the official language of the United States?

With an official language policy in the United States, we can give all citizens and immigrants the chance to master the English language and—

- secure equal opportunity for *all*
- create levels of social, economic, and political advancement that most immigrants could not have attained in their countries of origin
- assure full participation in the democratic process
- strengthen American business and the nation's economy, and
- make possible a greater sharing of cultural gifts and values among all our citizens.

Having an official language will require government responsibility for providing more opportunities for immigrants to learn English—as well as help them master civics requirements for naturalization. As these immigrants acquire full command of English, their chances for upward economic mobility will improve dramatically (as numerous studies have already shown).

Perhaps most important to society at large, having immigrants acquire English competency will give them a voice in the political process, *allowing for an even greater diversity of opinion in this country*.

Without an official policy, we can expect to see higher levels of unemployment among language minorities, more disparity between the positions employers wish to fill and workers seek to gain, and higher costs of remedial training and reeducation on the part of employers. In other words, the economy of the nation and every one of its citizens will suffer from the loss of language unity.

It's not difficult to imagine job applicants being turned away, not because they weren't qualified to perform the tasks required by the position, but because their English was insufficient to do business. It takes little imagination to envision a company losing profits because it can't find workers who speak English well enough to communicate with clients and customers.

It is also easy to envision the possibility of a national economy struggling to cope with a poorly educated work force not ready to take on the tasks of the 21st century.

These are easy ideas to accept—because in many ways they're already real.

U.S.ENGLISH seeks to pave the way for a better life for all Americans, "natives" and new immigrants alike. By *guaranteeing the right for all people living in the United States to learn English*, we will ensure that we are maximizing the talents and skills of all Americans in the work force.

Likewise, U.S.ENGLISH seeks to *make English the official language of government in the United States*, not only for the sake of efficiency in government, but also to ensure the same basic rights for all Americans.

U.S.ENGLISH has been waging effective campaigns in state and federal legislatures, working to pass laws protecting the language of equal opportunity for all Americans. U.S.ENGLISH legal experts have been in the courtrooms, fighting those who wish to relegate some members of our society to second-class citizenship. And U.S.ENGLISH has worked diligently to get the word out about official English in the media.

We will guarantee the existence of a politically unifying common language in the United States of America only by securing the passage of English Language Amendments and other key legislation on the state and federal levels. In recent years, great strides have been made and important victories won in the legislative arena. We still have a way to go, and U.S.ENGLISH will be at the forefront of these and other initiatives.

In the interim, too, U.S.ENGLISH continues to promote worthwhile education programs to teach English to immigrants. These programs will always be the cornerstone of all efforts to bring immigrants successfully into the mainstream of American society, so they can enjoy the fruits of democracy and economic freedom.

With more than 400,000 members nationwide, U.S. ENGLISH is one of the fastest-growing public interest groups in the nation. Momentum is gaining for official English—and we must keep up that momentum so that we can exert pressure on legislators and educators to make English a top priority.

I have lent my full support to U.S.ENGLISH. I am fully committed to its goals, and my commitment comes as a measure of my gratitude for all the United States of America has given to me. I ask you to consider what *you* have gained as a citizen of this extraordinary nation—and what you and all Americans stand to lose if the forces of language separatism prevail. Please join me in supporting U.S.ENGLISH so that this magnificent country, the greatest on the face of the earth, will continue as one nation, indivisible.

XI.

Postscript:
Immigrants' Impressions

What are the strongest impressions new immigrants have about the English language and American customs when they first arrive in the United States?

On learning the language:

Dinesh Desai, investment adviser, immigrated from India:
"Speech was the biggest problem for me. The Indians from whom I learned English in high school and college had strange accents and made quite different sounds in pronouncing English from what I found when I arrived, at 22, in America.

"I got off the ship in New York and immediately took a train to San Francisco. I sat next to a serviceman, and we repeatedly tried to start conversations with one another. Finally, we both gave up, because we couldn't understand one another's accents, expressions, manners—even a number of words. It was extremely frustrating!"

Asugman Atam, dentist, immigrated from Turkey:

"I didn't take much English in school or through formal English courses. I learned a lot while working and living here.

"I also listened to English tapes whenever I was in the car. And I would tape President Reagan's speeches on television and watch them over and over again, mouthing the words and expressions.

"This may sound like a strange way of putting it, but I feel that, because my husband and I weren't able to learn English quickly enough and well enough, we both lost two to three years in our professional careers. If we were to do it over again, we would certainly prepare ourselves with language much more thoroughly!"

Cynthia Tam, investment analyst, immigrated from Hong Kong:

"I had an experience not long ago that reminded me of my childhood nightmares with English. I was going to visit a friend in France, so I tried to learn some French before I went. I took flash cards with key phrases on them so that I would have something on me in case I got stuck.

"Well, the flash cards helped—but only to a limited extent. You see, even though I could get across my message by reading them the flash cards, I couldn't understand their answers! That reminded me a lot of our early days in America."

On making adjustments:
Dr. Atam:

"We like living like Americans, but we still hold to many of our Turkish customs."

Esther Eisenhower, educator:

"Language is no longer something you need for economic success—you now need it for economic *survival*.

Perhaps in the 1800s, you might have been able to get a job in a sweatshop or out in the fields and never have to learn English. In those days, immigrants could make it that way.

"Today, however, our economy has changed so much that it is no longer possible for most immigrants to operate this way. Our service-oriented society means we need people who can communicate with one another.

"We must insist on English literacy for new immigrants. It's a matter of *their* survival."

Their feelings about English:
Dr. Atam:

"My feeling is there should be an official language in the U.S. and it should be English. I even think English should be a *universal* language, since it is spoken all over the world."

Mr. Desai:

"The world has become much smaller through technology. I think it would be wonderful if we all spoke just *one* language, whatever that language might be.

"I would like to put in my bid for English, though. It is a tremendously versatile language. It seems to me that English is richer in vocabulary and expressiveness than almost any other language."

Stephen Baker, author, immigrated from Hungary:

"English is my second language, but my first love. It has a vocabulary twice the size of the next largest language, German. Yet it is also probably the most concise language in the world, requiring fewer words to say the same thing than in any other tongue. As I said in a recently published article on the subject, 'no doubt, English was invented in heaven. It must be the *lingua franca* of the angels. Nothing even comes close to it in sound, eloquence, and just plain common sense.' "

Long-term prospects:
Mr. Desai:
"I came to America with the idea that I'd eventually go back to India, but I was so transformed by America, so delighted with the society and the wonderful opportunities available here, that I soon changed my mind permanently. I'm here to stay!"

Mr. Baker:
"America is like one great big classroom for me."

* * * * *

Since I too am an immigrant to the United States, allow me to share with you my final thoughts on the issue of an official language for this country.

I've heard all the arguments for and against official English many times over. When the dust settles and I can see my own experience clearly, there are several basic truths I have discovered concerning language in this great nation we call the United States of America.

As a former attorney and orator, let me summarize the case for official English in the United States. I see *three reasons* for making the study of English in this country both mandatory and available to *all*:

The first concerns children, our most precious national resource. The most important communication we have is with our children—but perhaps we take this too much for granted. As many of the people in this book can tell you, terrible rifts often arise between immigrant parents and their children, caused or exacerbated by the lack of a common language.

We don't need *pachucos*, ethnic gangs, or other alienated youngsters who turn to the streets—even to crime and drugs

—just because their parents can't understand what they're saying.

We don't need the pain of parents who helplessly watch their children go down the tubes.

But we *do* need immigrant parents who can and will learn English in order to communicate with their children—and thereby provide the guidance and influence that *all* children so desperately need as they grow up.

That's the first reason for making English the official language of the United States: *to help keep our families together*.

The second has to do with isolation. I spent my early years in a Mexican mining town in which each group—Mexicans, Americans, British—lived in a compound surrounded by a barbed wire fence. The segregation was strictly enforced.

Later, I saw "colonies" like these when I was in Nicaragua as a graduate student, and I was repelled. This time, the segregation was deliberate, self-imposed. As in Panama, the colonies were not a legal fact but an expression of preference for isolation.

And, as in Panama, the results were ugly, unfair, and unjust.

By contrast, in the United States over the past 40 years, we've come to see how integration and assimilation have meant equal justice and better economic opportunity for *all* Americans. Isolation in America is a suicidal path for *any* group. We must guard against enticements such as "ethnic purity" or "cultural preservation"—which are often thinly veiled metaphors for isolation.

Ethnic leaders want to make us strangers in our own new land rather than *amigos*. But, as most immigrants will tell you, what *we* want most is to assimilate, to be friends and neighbors with other Americans of all races and religions.

Immigrants want to move forward just like everyone

everyone else. Let's not turn back the hands of time and regress to a harsher time when segregation, isolation, and injustice were the norm. Let us realize the great potential for ourselves and our nation by being one people with a common language.

So, the second reason for official English is *to keep our nation one and indivisible*.

My third reason is an offshoot of the second. By assimilation and integration, I do not mean we all need to act the same, wear the same clothes, eat the same foods, and have the same ideas. We are perhaps the most diverse nation in the world—nothing can take that away.

But with a common language, we can take advantage of this diversity to the greatest possible degree. We can understand our similarities and differences—and share more equitably in the great economic, cultural, and ethnic wealth of this nation.

Language makes this possible. Like music, language is a means of communication and the condition of harmony. To create a symphony of cultures, we must all follow the same conductor—and know what the conductor is saying to us and we to him.

That, ladies and gentlemen, is why I favor an official English policy in the United States—to preserve our families, our common humanity, and our diverse cultures. Language alone cannot accomplish these things, but without a common language, our chances of reaching these goals are very poor.

Fernando de la Peña

Contributors

Benefactors

Mr. John B. Bean
Ms. Margaret B. Branchflower
Mr. Edward R. Broida
Mr. Robert De Pree
   Patricia A. De Pree
Mrs. M. Deutschenschmied
Mr. F.M. Kirby
   F.M. Kirby Foundation, Inc.
Mrs. Marguerite Ladney
Mr. Charles Luckman
Mildred Lane Kemper Fund
Mrs. E.A. Newell
Mr. & Mrs. Allen H. Sanders
Dr. Thomas J. Stilp
   Polly Stilp
Weingart Foundation

Grantors

Ms. Patricia C. Acheson
Mr. Robert Allen
Amy Shelton McNutt Trust
Mr. & Mrs. R. Stanton Avery
Mr. Foster Bam
Miss Ruth Stevens Berry
Mrs. Helen B. Buckland
Mr. Pierre P. Claeyssens
Ms. Shirley I. Cowell
Mr. Elson L. Flora
Fred Stanback Inc.
Ms. Judith B. Friend
Mr. John Gray
Mr. & Mrs. John Gribbel 2nd
The Hahn Family Foundation
Harris Long Foundation
Dr. & Mrs. David T. Hellyer
Mrs. Doris Bice Heslip
Mr. Robert C. Hooper
Mr. Stanley S. Hubbard
Mr. & Mrs. Walter C. Klein
Mrs. John Langhorne
Mr. Bruno Leporati

Mr. & Mrs. J.W. Le Van
Mr. & Mrs. John F. Lott
Hon. Harold D. Martin (Ret.)
Mr. & Mrs. Frank M. Melton
North Star Foundation, Inc.
Mrs. Eugene Ormandy
Mr. M.P. Potamkin
Ms. Deborah Rokosz
Mr. & Mrs. Richard Rosenthal
   The Rosenthal Foundation
Mr. Randolph Rowland
Mr. David T. Schiff
   The Schiff Foundation
Mr. A. Thomas Shanks
Mrs. Frank C. Smith
Mr. William B. Snyder
Mrs. Stanley Stone
Mrs. Gera C. Terrell
Dr. Jocelyn Tomkin
Mrs. Evelyn Warner
Mr. Harold E. Willey
   Harold Willey Trust Fund
Mrs. Mabel Woolley

Patrons

Helen & Ted Anderson
Ms. Edith Marie Appleton
Dr. Harry L. Arnold, Jr.
Mrs. Audrey M. Auchincloss
Mr. Frederick E. Baer
Mr. C.K. Battram
Mrs. Betty Bean
D.J. Beaulieu
Mr. David O. Beim
Mrs. Moana Odell Beim
Mr. A. Benedict
Mr. Bruce Benson
 Benson Foundation
Mr. W.B. Browder
Mr. Thomas B. Calhoun
Mr. Philip L. Carret
Mr. & Mrs. David Chalmers
Mr. C. Thomas Clagett, Jr.
Mr. Robert Clark
Ms. Toni Cobb
Mr. William E. Collard
Mr. Albert R. Connelly
Mr. Alistair Cooke
Ms. Ursula Corning
Mrs. Lucile T. Daum
Mr. Joseph Di Maio
Mr. Fred Drexler
Mr. Ian M. Duncan
Mr. & Mrs. Frank R. Eyerly
Ms. Vera M. Falconer
Mrs. Alice C. Fick
Mr. Ralph Fine
Mrs. Shirley S. French
Mrs. Sylvia Furtick
Mr. J.M. George
 George Foundation
Mr. Donald R. Glancy
Mr. Joel M. Goldfrank
Mr. Norman Greenberg
Mr. Paul F. Heymann
Mr. David A. Horn
Irving Rothlein Foundation
Ms. Janet Ingram Kelly
Mrs. Elizabeth Knell-Shepard
Mr. H.J. Kip Koehler III

Mr. & Mrs. Lester C. Krogh
Mr. John Leslie
Ms. Margaret B. Long
Mr. James M. Lowerre
 Elizabeth A. Lowerre
Mrs. Sheldon R. Luce
Mr. John P. Marion
Mr. Sandro Mayer
Mr. Robert E. Messinger
Mr. J. Theodore Moody
Mr. John W. Moody
Mr. Frank F. Morrill
Mr. Robert Nalven
Ms. Mary V. Neff
Mr. S. Falck Nielsen
Mr. Joaquin M. Nin-Culmell
Mr. & Mrs. Donald E. Noble
Mrs. Lee Norris
Mr. Chauncey Norton
Mr. L. Allen Osborne
Mrs. Angie Papadakis
Mr. & Mrs. Spelman Prentice
Mr. Stanley E. Ragsdale
Mr. Daniel A. Richards
Mr. James T. Richards
Mr. & Mrs. E.B. Rickard
Mr. Robert G. Robinson
Mrs. Virginia M. Saalfield
Mr. Rowland Schaefer
Adm. Allen Mayhew Shinn, USN
Mrs. Margaret R. Shuttleworth
Mr. Frederic M. Sibley
Mr. Dean B. Smith
Mr. Gadsden Smith, Jr.
Mr. James B. Steere
Stephen L. Altshul Foundation
Mrs. Harley C. Stevens
Mrs. Helen R. Styer
Mr. Hugh B. Vanderbilt
Mr. Howard Van Vleck
Mr. Ronald M. Walker
Mrs. Roberta Lounsbury Warren
Mrs. Horton Watkins
Mr. James H. Wilson

Donors

Mr. Charles B. Abbot
Mr. George M. Acker
Adams Fund
Mr. & Mrs. Robert Adkins
Mr. Edward Ahrens
Alaska Services
Henry & Betty Albrecht Foundation
Mr. Gene Alderson
    Linda Alderson
Mr. David Alexander
Mr. & Mrs. Robert Alexander
Mr. Harper C. Allan
Mr. Robert B. Allan
Mrs. C. Robert Allen III
Mr. William R. Allen
Mr. & Mrs. William G. Allyn
Mrs. Charles S. Alter
Mr. Richard Alter
Mr. Ronald A. Alvarez
Mr. R.T. Amis
Mr. R.F. Ancha
Mrs. Arece L. Anderson
Mr. D.A. Anderson
Mrs. Geraldine Perry Anderson
Mr. Leo S. Anderson
Mr. Wm. Anderson
Mrs. Shirley Andoniades
R.A. Appell, M.D.
Mrs. D. Bradford Apted
Mr. & Mrs. Dino E. Argentini
Mr. Michael P. Arndt
Mr. Lewis Arno
Mr. Daryl W. Arnott
Mr. Francis J. Asti
Mr. & Mrs. Luther Avery
Mr. Frederick Bailey
Ms. Doris G. Baker
Mr. John A. Baker, Jr.
Rear Adm. Richard R. Ballinger, USN Ret.
    Virginia B. Ballinger
Mrs. June B. Bangham
Gregory Bard, M.D.
Dr. Jay G. Barnett
Mr. Sidney Baron

Mr. Andrew Barr
Mr. Harry Barrows
Mr. Francis E. Barse
    Ann Barse
Mr. Jacques Barzun
Mr. Charles K. Bates
Mrs. Harriett M. Bates
Mr. Alvin H. Baum, Jr.
Mr. Rogers Bayles
Mr. David L. Bean
Mr. B.B. Beebe
Mrs. Helen Beinecke
Mrs. Martha Bell
Mr. Ray Belnap
Mr. Reed Benedict
    Beverly J. Benedict
Miss Joan C. & Ann Benitt
Mr. Walter R. Bennett
Mr. William J. Berger
    Ruth K. Berger
Mr. W. Robert Berger
Dr. Robert B. Bergmann
Mrs. Ruth M. Berlin
Mr. Richard A. Bernstein
Mr. Eugene P. Bertin
Mr. Joe E. Best
Mr. Pierce H. Bitker
Mrs. S.R. Bjonerud
    Dorothy E. Talbot
Mr. John Bjorvik
Mrs. Mary V. Black
Mr. R. Gordon Black
Mr. William D. Blair
Mr. & Mrs. Henry Blankevoort
Mrs. Philip D. Block, Jr.
Mr. Glen H. Blomgren
    Gwen P. Blomgren
Mr. Eugene Boeke, Jr.
Mr. Dan M. Bogard
Mr. J.K. Bohannan
Mr. Robert G. Boice
Mrs. Ann M. Bolster
Mr. James C.H. Bonbright
Mr. Blaine M. Bonny

Dr. & Mrs. Burr H. Curtis
Ms. G. Marguerite Curtis
Mr. & Mrs. Maynard Cutler
Dr. James Cuykendall
Mr. Joshua P. D'Esposito
Mr. C. Dam
Mr. John Dannan III
Mrs. Joseph B. Danzansky
Mr. Thomas B. Darlington
Mr. Algirdas J. Dauginas
Mr. Keith W. Davidson
A. Grove Day
Mr. Don Day
Mr. Herbert L. Dean
Mrs. Betty De Beau
Mr. Charles A. Debenedittis
Mrs. Jenney De Groot Reuyl
Capt. Victor Delano
   Jacqueline Stinson Delano
Mrs. Rita E. Delfino
Mrs. Ruth Denison
Mr. James H. Deoms
Mr. Clarke De Waters
Col. Stanley Diamond
Mrs. George Dickson
Henry A. Diederichs, M.D.
Ms. Martha Stott Diener
Dr. Evelyn Dodge
Mr. Ernest Doebelin
   Geraldine M. Doebelin
Mr. Michael G. Dolin
Mr. Coleman Donaldson
Mrs. Evelyn A. Donaldson
Mrs. Lorna Doris Donnell
Mr. Ralph S. Dover
Ms. Betty J. Downey
Mrs. Virginia A. Doyle
Mrs. Alice B. Drake
Mr. H.W. Drescher
M.D. Dudash
William J. Duffy, M.D.
Mr. Douglas K. Dunn
Mr. John H. Dyett
Ms. Rose Dyson
Mr. S.F. Eannarino
Mr. W.H. Eaton
Mr. & Mrs. J.H. Egbers
Mrs. Helen Ehlers

Mr. & Mrs. Douglas R. Elder
Mr. Paul A. Elfers
Mr. Jack R. Elliott
Rear Adm. Robert W. Elliott, Jr.
Ms. P. Ferris Ellis
Ellison Educational EQ Inc.
Mr. J.H. Elsom
   Ann D. Elsom
Mr. Edward L. Emerson
Ms. Berenice Emrick
Mr. Max Endel
Mr. John Endriz
Mr. Jordan A. Engberg
Mr. & Mrs. Paul R. Enger
Mrs. Kathryn C. Englund
Mr. & Mrs. Louis R. Enlow
Mrs. Sarah G. Epstein
Mr. & Mrs. Urvan G. Epstein
Mr. Louis M. Ercsik
Ms. Luise Errol
Mrs. E. Mary Ewing
Mrs. Robert H. Ewing
Mr. & Mrs. Irwin L. Fabian
Mr. Arnold Fagen
Fred & Josephine Falkner
Harold F. Fallon
Mr. W.R. Farquhar
Lee E. Farr, M.D.
Mrs. John H. Fawcett
Mr. L. Federline
Mr. & Mrs. Eugene L. Fellner
Mr. Robert W. Felmlee
Mr. Alfred C. Fields
Mr. Allen E. Fine
Mrs. Liuba Firman
Mr. Carlos B. Fischer
James R. Fisher, Ed.D.
Mr. Berry Fleming
Dr. William H. Fleming
Brig. Gen. C.W. Fletcher
Mr. C.W. Flint, Jr.
Mr. Mike Fogle
Mrs. Peggy B. Foley
Mr. F. Richard Ford
Mr. & Mrs. Richard E. Ford
Mr. Dena Forster
C.R. Foss
Dr. William Fox

Ms. Katherine Francis
Ms. Geraldine Frederick
Mr. & Mrs. Donald H. Freeman
Mr. & Mrs. C. Norman Frees
Mrs. Julia Freitag
Alice D. Friedman, M.D.
Mrs. Betty Fritz
Mr. John H. Fritz
Lt. Col. Elbert E. Fuller, Jr., USA Ret.
Mr. C.E. Fultz
Mr. & Mrs. Edward Furash
Mrs. Merle Gahagan
Mrs. M. Lee Gaillard
Mrs. Henry J. Gaisman
Mr. R.L. Gallagher
Mr. Herbert Gallin
Mrs. Hilda D. Gantt
Ms. Martha B. Gardner
Mrs. Dotti Garrett
Mr. D.K. Garrison
Mrs. Geoffrey S. Garstin
Mr. Marshall Garth
   Martha B. Garth
Miss E.S. Gauntt
Mr. Richard Gaustad
Ms. Maria C. Geier
Rabbi Everett Gendler
Mr. John E. Gerli
Mr. Gilbert S. Getlin
Mr. Ivan A. Getting
Ms. Coline M. Gibbons
Dr. W. Russell Gibson
Mr. C.C. Giddens, Jr.
Mr. Robert K.W. Gideon
Mr. Porter W. Gifford
Mrs. Nancy S. Gillespie
Mr. John J. Gilman
Mr. David D. Gilpatrick
Mr. E.W. Gilson
Mrs. Reynolds Girdler
Glazier Fund
Mr. Francis H. Gleason
Dr. John C. Glenn, Jr.
Mrs. Anne Gold
Mr. Vernon L. Goodin
Mrs. Rebecca G. Goodman
Mrs. Elma L. Goodwin
Mr. A. Louise Gordon

Mr. H. Edward Gordon
Ms. Melissa Gordon
Mr. Paul R. Goudy
   Fay L. Goudy
Mrs. H. Gow
Mr. Charles P. Grahl
Mr. Paul A. Grannas
Mr. Nelson Gray
Dr. Robert F. Gray
Mrs. Marilyn Ratliff Greb
Mr. Earl L. Green
Mr. Leon D. Green
Miss Sydney S. Green
Dr. & Mrs. William R. Green
Mr. Sherwood R.H. Greenwell
Col. Clifford C. Gregg
Mrs. Golda Gregg
Mr. Barron Grier
Ms. Keating Griffiss
Mr. William Grohne
Mr. Frank J. Gross
Dr. Lawrence R. Gurin
Mr. Eric Gustafson
Mr. Arthur C. Guyton
   Ruth W. Guyton
Mr. Howard J. Gysin
Ms. Alice Hague
Mr. Alexander S. Haig
Mr. M.H. Halderson
Mr. Bart Hall
Mr. Robert S. Hansel
Mr. Edwin Hansen
Mrs. John J. Harding
Mrs. Sandra S. Harris
Mrs. Karla K. Harrison
Lawrence P. & Oletha G. Hart
Mr. Carl Hartdegen
Ms. Lenora F. Harth
Mr. Paul Harvey, Jr.
Mr. Thomas B. Harvey
Mr. F.K. Haslund, Jr.
Mr. Jack W. Hawkins
Mrs. William H. Hazlett
Mr. Milton W. Heath, Jr.
Mr. Arthur R. Heckerman
Mr. Pierre V. Heftler
Mr. Robert G. Heitz
Mr. A.C. Helmholz

Mr. Gates M. Helms
Mr. Andy L. Henderson
Dr. Edward D. Henderson
Mr. & Mrs. George W. Henry
Mr. W.L. Henry
Mrs. Arthur L. Herberger
Mrs. Grover M. Hermann
Dr. James Herzog
Mr. Herbert Hezlep III
Mr. Richard J. Hicks
  Letty L. Hicks
Ms. Hiden
Mr. William A. Higgins
Ms. Ruth Hilliard
Mr. Endocen H. Hillman
Mr. Scott Hinsdale
Mr. Kenneth Hinsvork
Mr. Wm. G. Hintz
Mr. John T. Hitchcock
Mr. W.F. Hocker
Mr. Frederick Holdsworth, Jr.
Mr. James Holly
Mrs. Jean T. Hooper
Mr. Howard V. Horne
Mrs. C.B. Hortenstine
Richard & Sheila Horton
Mr. P. Householder
Ms. Mary E. Hovestad
Mrs. E. Carol Hubbard
Mr. Glenn R. Hubbard
Mr. Donald A. Hubner
Dr. & Mrs. Page Hudson
Ms. Josephine F. Huey
Mrs. Rosemarie Hughes
Mr. Roy Hughes
Mr. T. Edgar Hughes
Mr. Carl Hunt
Mr. Charles F. Hyde
Mr. John A. Ilibassi
Mr. Joseph M. Imparato
Lily & Robert Ireland
Mr. Herbert M. Iris
Mr. & Mrs. David Irish
Mr. William Irish
Lt. Col. Gerard B. Isaacs
Dr. Anthony D. Ivankovich
Mr. Orren Jackson
Rev. Fred Jacobsen

Mr. R.I. Jacobson
Mr. Frank J. Janarek
Mr. James L. Janes
Mr. Jerry Frank Jelen
Ms. Marion E. Jemmott
Mr. Dave Jenks
Mrs. E. Lee Jens
Mr. Robert S. Johanson
Mrs. Charlotte Johnson
Ms. Dorothy Gerriets Johnson
Mrs. E.T. Johnson
Mrs. Florence S. Johnson
Mrs. Lillian B. Johnson
Mr. Luther B. Johnson, Jr.
Mr. Lenard Johnston
Mr. Richard Johnston
Mrs. Christene Clark Jones
Mr. & Mrs. Jennings A. Jones
Mr. John W. Jones
Mr. Morgan Jones
Mr. R.I. Jones
Mr. & Mrs. Wayne V. Jones
Mr. Carl E. Jorgensen
Mrs. Ellen W. Josephson
Mr. Jonathan K. Kahananui
Mr. E.J. Kahn, Jr.
Dr. & Mrs. Fredrick H. Kahn
Mr. Herbert Kahn
Lt. Col. William A. Kalberer
  Carol M. Kalberer
Ms. Shirley N. Kaleth
Mr. Howard E. Kambach
Dr. & Mrs. Milton A. Kamsler, Jr.
Mr. Arthur G. Karlstedt
Mr. S.M. Katz
Dr. & Mrs. J.V. Richard Kaufman
Mr. Thomas T. Kawano
Mr. D.R. Kearney
Mr. Lawrence Kelly
Ms. Elizabeth M. Kennedy
Dr. & Mrs. Thomas D. Kerenyi
Mr. Bruce M. Kerner
Miss Justine Kerstock
Mrs. Lucille M. Kiernan
Mr. Robert S. Kieve
Mr. W. Killgallon
Mr. Jerrold L. Kingsley
Mr. William E. Kirkland

Mr. James E. Palmer
Mr. Robert L. Palmer
Mrs. Frances C. Palmquist
Mrs. Edith S. Pankratz
Lt. Col. Peter G. Pappas
Mr. F.C. Parcell, Jr.
Mr. John C. Parish
Mr. Kenneth W. Park
Mrs. Lee I. Park
Mr. Leo J. Parry, Jr.
  Roberta Parry
Ms. Beatrice Parsons
Mrs. Wallace K. Patton
Dr. Milton O. Peach
Mr. Blaine Pearl
Mr. Robert W. Pearson
Mr. Edson R. Peck
Mr. Norman E. Pehrson
Mrs. Eugenia B. Pellizzon
Mr. John Penhallow
Peninsula Republican Women Federated
Dr. Paul F. Peppard
Dr. F.D. Pepper, Jr.
Mr. Jack T. Perrine
Ms. Margaret H. Perry
Rev. William A. Perry
Mr. E. Leslie Peter
Mr. Jay L. Peters
Mr. Thomas Petrone, Jr.
Mr. James T. Pettus, Jr.
Mr. Richard P. Pfiffner
Mrs. Barbara Murray Philips
Ms. A. Irene Pollard Phillips
Mr. E.L. Phillips
Mr. Thomas A. Phillips, Jr.
Mr. & Mrs. Thomas N. Phillips
Mr. Arthur G. Pierdon
Mr. John S. Pillsbury
Mr. Hugh R. Pingree
Mr. L. Don Pipe
Lt. Col. (Ret.) & Mrs. Joseph T. Piscotta
Mr. & Mrs. A.L. Pittinger
Mr. Donald L. Poggi
Mr. Wayne C. Ponader
Mr. John C. Pope
Mrs. Rickman Powers
Mr. Cliff Pratt
  Edith Pratt

Mrs. H. Irving Pratt
Mr. Charles B. Preston
Mrs. Constance S. Pritchard
Mr. M.P. Pusack
Mr. James T. Pyle
Mr. H.L. Quintana
  Vera M. Quintana
Mr. Wilbur M. Rabinowitz
Mr. Edmund Radkiewicz
Mr. John A. Radway, Jr.
Mr. M.L. Raiser
Mrs. Judith S. Randal
Bernard J. Ransil, M.D.
Mr. & Mrs. Norman Rappoport
Mr. Wilbert Rath
Mr. Louis J. Rauch
Mr. Phillip Rauch
Mrs. Yvonne Raup
Mr. Allen Walker Read
Mr. O.H. Reaugh
Ms. Martha Reckdahl
Mr. & Mrs. Maurice A. Reidy, Jr.
Mr. Chester J. Renard
Mrs. Marjorie Renegar
Mrs. Stewart Resch
Miss Julia R. Reynolds
Mr. L.E. Rhian, Sr.
Mr. Robert E. Rhine
Mr. Henry H. Rice
Mrs. Bartlett Richards
Mr. Tom Richards
Mr. Guy D. Richardson
Mr. Daniel M. Ricker, Jr.
Mr. George T. Rideout, Jr.
Mr. & Mrs. F.B. Riechmann
Mr. Fred W. Riggs
  Clara-Louise Riggs
Mr. & Mrs. Jock Ritchie
Mr. Stoyell M. Robbins
Mr. Frederic M. Roberts
Ms. R.H. Roberts
Mr. Stuart Robertson
Mr. James E. Robison
Mrs. Richard Rodgers
  Richard & Dorothy Rodgers
  Foundation
Mr. B.W. Rogers
Mrs. Priscilla B. Rogers